Conversational
RAPE

Revised Edition

Dr. Pat Allen's groundbreaking approach
to help you get what you want in life by healing
trauma from negative language experiences
and changing the words you speak
to change the way you think.

CONVERSATIONAL RAPE

Emotional Language, Conditional Love and Invasive Communication Patterns

by Pat Allen, PhD, LMFT, CAS
Founder, WANT® Institute

Revised Edition

Conversational Rape (Revised Edition)
Emotional Language, Conditional Love and Invasive Communication Patterns
© 2012 The Dr. Pat Allen WANT® Institute
3355 Via Lido, Suite 205, Newport Beach, CA 92663
Original Edition published 1980

ISBN 978-0-9824808-2-3

Printed and bound in the United States of America

First Printing — May 2012

The WANT® Institute is a nonprofit 501(c)(3) California Corporation operating for educational, scientific and charitable purposes. The WANT® Institute is also a Federally Registered and Approved Health Care provider, National Provider Identifier (NPI) 1912034216.

Cover design, text design, layout and production by Edward Rapka.
This book was typeset in classic Goudy.

CONTENTS

ACKNOWLEDGEMENTS

I want to thank and acknowledge the following loving people
for their part in helping and supporting me in writing this book:
Mark Herron, who edited the original manuscript,
Gary Patton who created the wonderful cartoon illustrations,
and Tom Lord who first suggested the title
at Thanksgiving Dinner 1979.

I also deeply appreciate the work of Jim Hallowes who facilitated
getting this revised edition back into print and the insights
he's taught me about highly sensitive people.
I appreciate the creative efforts of Edward Rapka.
And I especially want to acknowledge all of the many years my
daughter Sue Wagner has devoted to helping me build my MFT
practice, including helping to distribute all of my books
and educational products.

Last but not least, I acknowledge all that I have learned from all the
clients who have believed in my work. Thank you all.

Dedicated to H.P.

Published by

WANT® INSTITUTE
Educators of Effective Communication Strategies

Speak Rationally.

Decide Rationally.

Disagree Rationally.

PREFACE

The term rape is ordinarily used in reference to the physical, sexual violation of another human being. There are other forms of rape which violate the mind and spirit of a human being in ways which may or may not leave physical marks. Jails and mental hospitals are full of people who bear no physical marks to show the rape which has taken place. This more subtle form of rape I have termed *Conversational Rape*.

All humans are born with the potential to feel through the body senses of taste, touch, smell, sight, and hearing.

Humans think symbolically through imagery and/or dreams and words. Psychological stability, social interaction abilities, deductive and inductive reasoning, and problem solving capability (IQ), are all significantly determined by language abilities.

When this language training begins around one or two years of age, the motivation behind the training will be based on one of two types of love. One is unconditional, acceptance love which recognizes the rights of the little child to have any and all feelings, wants and not-wants, and to express them. The second restricts the child to "right and wrong" feelings, shoulds and should-nots. In this latter language program, conditional love is given for good performance.

The child, in order to survive in the family unit, soon learns to activate negative processes. Whether suppression, repression, projection, sublimation or compensation, these processes cloak the child's true feelings and thoughts, rather than allow for their free expression.

Through this language training program, the personality and identity of both the trainer parent and the trainee child blend together to perpetuate a system which systematically rapes both of their true feelings, thoughts, and free actions. It is more a reaction "should" program, than an action "want" program. The resulting behavior has been labeled gamey, neurotic, and/or psychotic.

Conditionally loved children have been psychologically raped by intimidation through fear of abandonment and/or rejection. The physically battered child is the ultimate gamey rape but the nonphysical psychological rape which is perpetuated through language — both verbal and non-verbal — can be as violent to the mind and spirit as the physical rape is to the body.

Language is significantly taught in the first five years of life and the basic program is perpetuated all during life. Each feeling, thought and action uses language as a vehicle of communication to oneself and to others. If the basic language training system was based on intimidation and seduction ("Do it or else I will not love you" or "Do it for me and I will love you more"), the person will believe that this conditional love system is the right way to do it. He or she will adopt the system as the norm, and use it throughout their life, thus perpetuating more intimidation and seduction, and more conversational rape.

I have written this book for two reasons. The first is to identify and quantify those factors that drive persons into destructive communication patterns that cause pain and inhibit intimacy in human relationships. The second is to describe and share an approach to communication and language that I have personally developed and tested successfully throughout my career as a marriage and family therapist and a clinical Transactional Analyst. The techniques that will be presented will enable both other therapists and individuals at large to diagram ego states and to channel feelings through a rational thinking process which relies solely on the control of personal language.

Through language behavior modification, an individual will gradually learn how to think about what he or she wants and doesn't want in life, how to protect physical, mental and emotional interpersonal rights without resorting to the use of hostile or defensive tactics, and how to understand the ways in which the family traditions with which one was raised have subconsciously both positively and negatively influenced behavior into adulthood.

I will also show how to develop communication skills which focus on strengthening the positive (assertiveness) and eliminating the negative (discounts) in interpersonal exchanges.

My basic assumption in all of this work has been that. for the most part, man's basic nature is good. A bias toward goodness exists in almost all persons, however it has to be found and fostered through the intellect.

My purposes in writing this book are as follows:

1. To show the influence of language training and communication systems on human beings from embryo to grave.

2. To demonstrate how humans have been conversationally raped themselves and how they in turn rape others.

3. To raise the reader's awareness of the role language use plays in relationships and convey new ideas on how to recognize the negative ploys of intimidation and seduction in communication, and thereby avoid the rape consequences.

4. To teach the reader how to love themselves and others better, particularly little children who are in a very vulnerable state of development.

5. To help make this a more loving world in which we all can live successful and productive lives.

A GLEAM IN DADDY'S EYE

Conversation

PREGNANT MOM:
   I hate being pregnant.

DAD:
   You were the one that said you couldn't
   get pregnant.

MOM:
   Why is it everything is always my fault?

RAPE!

1

Rape Analysis

Here is a case of a man and a woman engaged in conversational rape because of anger and guilt. She is complaining about being a pregnant victim of a man. He is attempting to alleviate his guilt by dumping the responsibility back on her. The circle of strife continues; she gets hostile and defensive.

Conversational rape is a combination of seduction and intimidation, with these people manipulating, in a gamey way, for both power and strokes.

The real victim in this rape is the unborn child living within the anxious, cortisol-adrenalized body of the woman.

It is this little human who receives the true messages of negativity passing through mother. Baby perceives and thinks in pure sensations of pain and pleasure without benefit of thinking symbolically with words or images. Baby records these negative perceptions on his/her neurological system as the foundation of his/her reality.

Should this negative behavior continue, such a "pain centered" human may become a "pain addict." Comfort will be available only with the experience of physical, mental, or emotional pain. Discomfort will arrive whenever too much pleasure is apparent.

On the other hand, baby may be the person choosing to become a "no-pain addict." This person continually avoids pain as if it could kill them. However, the "no-pain addict," anxious to "stuff" or "suppress" their pain, drinks excessively, over eats, or indulges in drugs or sex. Believing they are escaping destruction, they are in reality promoting it.

When we lose pleasure significantly at birth, we then become mistrusting of pleasure. We become more aware of feelings, deciding it to be an unreliable system, and move up into our heads — thinking. Such people actually become "pain centered." Pain is polarized, and they gravitate to one extreme or the other — towards pain or away from it.

The parent-centered home seeks retribution for the parent and the baby is forced to live in that environment. The parents have deprived feelings and they resent the baby's interference with their need for strokes to counter that deprivation.

In a child-centered home, the parents have been at one time well-gratified children. Therefore they pass this on to their babies, and their babies are well-gratified. By generously touching, by generously loving, by feelings that surround the baby, by the "vibes," and by responding to the baby's needs, the baby's feelings receive priority.

Straight Talk

Straight talk in this situation would involve the Mommy and Daddy in a search for ways to gratify each other, in order for them to give generously to the baby. Then the baby would naturally learn to turn this feeling back and the positive energies generated form a complete circle in the cycle.

The first solution for this situation is for Mother to embark on a good prenatal program. Physically, she makes certain that her body is well-loved and nurtured. She is careful about nutrition, exercise, and weight. Mentally, she controls her environment in comfortable ways. This will help her to deal with problems as they arise. Her mind should continually nurture her, reminding her to mother herself and receive mothering through her mental processes. Mother's mind will not trigger anxiety if she receives the support she needs in her environment. Emotionally, mother sees to it that she experiences a maximum of pleasure because the anxious body has a tendency to put out toxic chemicals which have a very negative effect on the nervous system.

The nervous system is the communication center between mother's body and baby's body. What Mother puts out in the way of neurological messages will be sent to that baby. Good prenatal programs — physical, mental, and emotional — are of paramount importance for the child.

Also, Mother should receive a childbirth system in which the mother and the baby work together in a pleasure-centered way to the greatest degree possible, so that the baby maximizes the pleasurable experience of the birth process.

Measurement of the birth process in terms of pain and/or pleasure has much to do with mother's anxiety level. Being educated in the birth process, feeling good about the process taking place, helps mother relax her body enough to provide the most pleasure-centered transition phase for the baby, going from the uteral to postpartum state.

Birth Without Violence, by Dr. Frederick Leboyer (Alfred A. Knopf, 1975), is the poignant statement about a pleasure-centered birth process. For an awareness of the extreme damage that can be done, Arthur Janov's *Primal Scream* is a statement of concern over the physical, mental, and emotional trauma of birth.

And so, after a good prenatal program, and a sensitive birth system, baby is launched into the world. It is of extreme importance, as Dr. Leboyer outlines, that skin-to-skin contact is achieved as soon as possible. This grounds the baby with maximum physical contact. It is the initiation of the communications system of body-to-body, touch-to-touch (feeling-to-feeling), and the moment of first skin-to-skin contact is when and where grounding takes place.

Everything that you have experienced to the point of sufficient neurological development is still there in our memory and serves as a source of pain or pleasure. If Mommy and Daddy will see that baby's needs are met on a consistent and child-centered basis, that baby will become what we call psychologically superior. Baby will have a significant, profound, and deep belief in its right to exist in this world. With a place in the sun, with people seen as primary sources of pleasure, identity is available.

If people aren't sources of pleasure, baby will pull away from the reality of people into the world of inanimate objects and intangible activities…eating, drinking, and often excessive consumerism.

Everyone needs strokes — negative or positive, kisses or kicks — in order to satisfy their stimulation stroke hunger. When Mommy and Daddy engage in a conversation which attempts to elicit negative, gamey strokes, they are gratifying their stroke hunger. Their actions speak to the fact that they were taught this way as children, and now they are passing the same system on to their child.

In order to talk straight, mommy and daddy must first learn that being critical of each other indicates a lack of unconditional accepting love of themselves first, and each other second. We give to each other what we give to ourselves. Therefore, it is important to love ourselves and then share that love with others through good, straight communication.

In this dialogue between pregnant mother and soon-to-be father, a loving communication would have been as follows:

Rational Conversation

PREGNANT MOM:
>Honey, I want to talk to you about how I feel being pregnant. Are you willing to talk now or later?

DAD:
>It's fine now. (or) We can talk later.

MOM:
>I accept my responsibility for mistakenly believing I was protected from pregnancy. I also know that you did not intend to cause me pain by getting me pregnant. However, I really feel negative at this time and want us to talk from time to time about my feelings so we can deal with them positively. I want to feel good and I want my baby to feel wanted. Are you willing to share my feelings?

DAD:
>Honey, I know we goofed in getting you pregnant at this time, but I do want you and the baby to feel good because I care about you both. I am willing to talk from time to time about your negative feelings. If I don't want to talk, I'll tell you straight. I don't want to play games with you. I love you.

With this kind of communication, both Mother and Dad are expressing their feelings and handling them appropriately. Baby benefits by having a nurturing mother's body in which to live, thus promoting good chemical communication between them.

BABY TALK

Conversation

BABY:
Waaaauuuuuggghh!!

MOTHER (to friend):
Oh, she's spoiled. She always cries like that at this time. I let her cry it out; it's good for her lungs.

BABY:
[More CRYING, eventually CRYING himself or herself to sleep, or baby gets a spanking and then cries himself or herself to sleep].

MOTHER:
See I told you she would stop.

RAPE!

Rape Analysis

Baby and Mom have participated in conversational rape. Baby is crying in order to seduce Mom into stroking her. Mom withholds strokes, intimidating the baby to give up and go to sleep without strokes. Further, if the child is one, two or three years old Mother may even go in and spank the child, unfortunately enhancing a negative stroke system, and reinforcing for both an overall negative stroke economy.

"She's spoiled." Mom's statement discounts the child as not being okay. "She's spoiled" is a critical, non-nurturing, non-loving, ultimately negative rape message. Mother, were she really a generous mother, would say, "She may be okay, she always cries like that; and when she does, I respond to her." Mother love, which may be physical and/or mental, is unconditional.

The age-old rocking motion involved in mothering is very important for the baby. In effect the rocking motion causes vestibular stimulation for the child. Neurological response, and hence neurological development, one of the last stages of the baby's development is maximized. A caring and consistent mother who rocks, holds, and carries her baby, thereby insuring a neurologically well-grounded infant, is helping to guarantee her child a life with less physical, mental, and emotional problems.

In support of these thoughts, researchers indicate that our "touch hunger" is absolute. Further, researchers actually quantify touch hunger with the simple identifying quotient that well-touched people are satisfied human beings. Infants in contact with mother's body through the strapping or holding stages become pleasure-centered adults who know how to stroke both themselves and other people positively.

The first three months of the child's life, before either symbolic imagery or abstract cognition takes place, are especially important in this mother-infant contact. The goal is for the baby to have a good "people stroke" economy, the result of fulfilling the touch hunger quotient.

Here is another scene between parents and a young child, now three years old. It is bedtime and the child is playing:

MOTHER:
  It's time to go to bed now.

CHILD (fussing):
  I want to play some more.

MOTHER:
  No, I said now! Do you want Daddy to spank you?

CHILD:
  Waaaauuuuuggghh!!

MOTHER:
  Okay, just a little longer.

RAPE!

Rape Analysis:

In this case, mother, baby, and mentioned father indicate rape. Baby is learning to distrust people, leading to a loss of security. Inconsistent parenting and the loss of security leads to instability. The lack of trust is also a source of information about pain rather than pleasure.

Mother exercises rape, exhibiting a lack of security in herself to be a stable giving person. She doesn't trust her own thinking, indicating a past rape of her own thinking process. In turn, mother passes the rape to father, setting him up as the "Bogey Man" in the child's life, the bearer of pain.

If Dad accedes to Mom and spanks the child on her say-so, he is allowing himself to be raped through emotional intimidation. If he does not cause the child pain, Dad will receive pain from Mother (wife).

By the age of three, baby has become cognitive, aware of symbolism. Mother's face is a symbol of pleasure. Going to bed is an awareness of loss of pleasure. Baby has become aware of the thought processes, including a memory, that indicate some actions are pleasurable and some are painful.

Pain and pleasure are both normal and natural concepts. They are feelings, and as such, non-negotiable. Feelings exist, period… they are neither good nor bad. It is the exercise of those feelings, what you do with them, that counts. What you do with your feelings shows whether you are a rational or an emotional person.

Rational people have been taught early on that "Yes, pain exists." However, the teaching they received incorporated the stable advice that effective use of the brain will allow an appropriate action to be taken. Naturally, baby goes toward pleasure and away from pain. Bed is painful, playing is pleasurable. Since Mother and Father are pain addicts; i.e., they are either habituated to pain or afraid of pain themselves, they allow the baby to dominate the home for the sake of gratification. The baby is being spoiled, developing an inability to deal with pain.

Mother shows her fear of pain. She doesn't want to anger the child, probably because she's afraid of the pain the baby will bring her. She feels insecure in facing that pain, so she avoids it and passes it on to Dad. In effect however, her transfer unreasonably gratifies baby's pleasure want; doing so, she sets no price on the behavior herself. The growing child is left without encouragement toward self-discipline.

The child learns or becomes aware that under all conditions we have to have pleasure. Pain to the child is seen as destructive and negative. Pain is bad. Painful experiences are bad. The discipline of mother is lacking because she fears causing pain. She is setting up a system of conditional loving, *i.e.*, "If you do this, then I will love you," or "If you do that, I will not love you." In this case, Mother is saying, "If you don't cry or fuss, I'll love you."

The child, a victim of inconsistent parenting, naturally starts to set up a system. "Mother lets me stay up. Therefore, Mother loves me." And the opposite of that is "Father makes me go to bed; Father requires me to perform; Father does not pay attention to my feelings; therefore, Father doesn't love me."

The child learns to establish a full system of "no-pain." These parents, also wishing a no-pain environment, stress performance at the expense of feeling. The *singular process of pleasure* has taken precedence over the *balance of all feelings* maintained in a pleasure-centered way. Without this balance, an uneven ratio develops, foundations for harmful systems are laid, and problems result in later life.

On the opposite extreme, what if the large, big, adult-sized members of the family have been raised in an emotional way themselves? What if these adults have been raised to feel their feelings and react spontaneously to their feelings, thinking only later of the results? This ill balanced pattern adds up to chaos, and the child loses faith in people as a source of true information.

As a result, the child learns to pull away from human beings and gravitates toward trustable *objects*. Very often, these trustable objects might be totally invested in a world beyond reality, a world of daydreaming, fantasy, and imaginary people.

It is not inconceivable to state, then, that children we call "brains" have developed an addiction to books as a source of strokes. The books are "object" strokes because the brainy child has lost faith in human beings. He or she may be brighter than the other people around them or they may be unable to obtain positive strokes from their families.

If young children under five years old are raised in a totally emotional, spontaneous way, the ultimate price tag will be what I call a pain-centered personality. The child refuses to seek pleasure because pleasure is a no-no in their family. They only perform. They only work. Life is for trudging. They become the game players of the world. Or, they become the total *process*-centered person who believes life is to be lived spontaneously, never mind what your head says the price will be. Spontaneity produces chaos. Self-discipline allows for spontaneity. Mother and Father are models of self-discipline. Self-discipline means, "I feel my feelings, I think my thoughts, and I act on them rationally."

Straight Talk

What would be the straight talk in these situations? In the first case, if Mother wants to be a balanced nurturing mother, she will decide what performances are best suited for the ultimate good of the baby. She will, in a nurturing way, see that those performances are done, while taking into account baby's feelings or processes. Mother might find loving ways to negotiate with the young child. A suggestion is "I'll rock you for a little while, and then you'll go to bed." Or take an inanimate object, a timer is a particularly good one, and say to baby, "I'll set the timer, and when the timer goes off, then you will go to bed." Be sure to set the timer!

There are also loving suggestions that have existed for thousands and thousands of years. "Mother will read/tell you a story before you go to bed." and "Mother will sing to you before you go to bed." The performance of your actions or words should be that of a loving person. Feelings are tended, thinking is encouraged, and the consequent behavior takes into account both feelings and thinking.

With our older, more aware three year old, a straight talk, go-to-bed dialogue might be as follows:

Rational Conversation

MOTHER:
It's time to go to bed now.

CHILD:
No! I want to play some more.

MOTHER:
I know it's fun to play and I will set the
timer so you can play a little longer.
(Timers are impartial) When it goes off,
I want you to go to bed without crying.
Will you do that?

CHILD:
Yes. (Or, "No." If no, then Mother elicits more
talk until child understands and agrees.)

If necessary, Mother promises a "prize" for performing, which may be a promise of quality together time when child wakes up. Or, Mother may set a pricetag on resistance, such as privilege, TV, bike ride, or visit to grandparents.

Either way, the child is being instructed in how to integrate and process feelings and thinking with his/her acting performance. Mother is also demonstrating her abilities to integrate her feelings, her thoughts, and her actions as a role model for the child. Further, Mother is showing her willingness to be a negotiable human being. She is encouraging the child to develop his/her own thinking, decision-making processes.

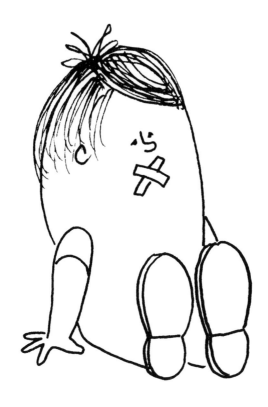

CHILDREN SHOULD BE SEEN
AND NOT HEARD

Conversation

CHILD:
(Grade-School age, presenting an
average report-card...)

MOM/DAD:
(By word or behavior)
You could have done better.

CHILD:
(Sad) I did my best.

MOM/DAD:
That's not good enough.

RAPE!

3

Rape Analysis

Where is the rape in this case? The dialogue exhibits parents who have themselves been raised in a performance-centered home. Their own parents' wishes were more important than their comfort. This system of performance over process is now important to them as parents.

These parents not only view thinking as more important than feeling, they also see the actual behavior as more important than feeling good.

These parents were raped as children and now do the same to their own child. In this example dialogue, the child is convinced that he/she has done the best that can be expected. The parents are essentially replying in discount, saying: "That's not good enough. We're okay; we did it for our parents. Since you're not doing it for us, you're not okay."

Straight Talk

What would be a more appropriate exchange between parents and child? First, prior to analysis of the report card, parents need to take into account what they know about the child's academic capability. Is the child slow, average, or bright? After acknowledging the child's capability, those parents who want to motivate the child toward better performance may use the prize system. The prize is not exactly a bribe, it is an appropriate form of motivation. If a pay check can be considered bribery, our lives are spent giving and taking bribes. However, the lack of it leaves us in a deprived state. Simply stated, we are rewarded for our efforts throughout our lifetimes. Certainly then, parents who want to promote performance will do well to reward — they will do well to give prizes to their children for appropriate behavior.

Are the parents in the position to operate such a reward system? Are they able to feel self-stroked so that they are not living vicariously through the child? Are the parents comfortable with their own lives, their own systems? If these parents are able to *feel good* about themselves, then they are what I call Peer Parents, parents who avoid playing one up and one down with each other.

Peer Parents negotiate with their children based on the tangible reward. For some parents, notions of prices and prizes conjure up some mystical malevolence. These are the parents who insist to the child, "I want you to do so because I say so." In effect, these parents are putting egoistic pressure on children to be altruistic. These parents see the Peer Parent statement, "I want you to do so because this or that will happen," as being control, i.e., bad! Prices and prizes are seen as being not "meaningful."

Is this truly the case in life? Certainly when we're little we tend to want our strokes to come in concrete, observable, sensuous, situation-response ways…candy, prizes, or goodies. As we mature, we still want strokes, though a simple pat on the head or a verbal affirmation may fill the bill.

There is a false pride on the part of parents who point to the maturity of the children, exhibited by the child's obedient response to the simple statement: "I want you to do it."

In point of fact, "I want you to do it," is **you *should* do it.** Performance is taking precedence over process. Think about that statement, the parent telling the child, "I want you to do it." Behind this ostensibly mature instruction is the following kind of thinking:

"I don't care that you feel intimidated. I don't care that I am motivating you through fear of being either rejected or abandoned by me. In fact, I'm going to convince Grandma and Grandpa and everyone in the neighborhood that you did it because you are such a good kid."

To this add, "No one will ever know that what I've done is totally intimidate and rape you into doing it, that there has been no negotiation. I wanted you to do it, and you did it, period."

These families that suppress the expression of wants in favor of performance shoulds, may, on the surface, be heralded as "polite." However, the extremely polite child grows up facing an impotence in determining his or her own wants. Do they know what they want, where they want to go, what they want to do, how they want to do it? The child, in pleasing the I-want-you-to-do-it parent, is rewarded from birth through age eighteen. From eighteen onward, however, they are punished through lack of self-gratifying reward, and often need extensive therapy.

Politeness is important, but inappropriate when it is an outgrowth of a family that practices intimidation-rape. The response of the child is, "I'll do it your way because you know more about it." In effect, surface politeness is seen and consequently rewarded. However, *should* is being stressed over *want*.

Peer Parents know that children are children and that, mercifully, good children strokes need only be simple prizes or very simple concrete prices. This system does not lead to the "spoiled" child. Spoiled means the child receives everything he or she wants because the child or parent is incapable of dealing with the element of pain. The child must have the human right to negotiate with the parents. The child must be able to state what he or she wants. But the very act of negotiation equates with the fact that the child may or may not get what they want. The child is not spoiled when pain is seen simply as an element/feeling with which he or she must deal.

The major premise of this book is that the language we use indicates how okay we are. The parental language trainer conversationally rapes the child by saying, "You should do it because I say so. Parents are more important than kids." The beginning of a conversational rape has commenced coincidentally with the beginning of language training.

Very quickly after birth, babies begin to convert their pure feelings of pain and pleasure into symbols representing these thoughts and feelings. By the age of one to two, they have picked up words and meanings which label their thoughts and feelings.

Those people who are responsible for teaching these words and meanings to the young child in effect control the child's communication skills within and outside the child's head. The impact of this control is far-reaching.

If the adult in charge is himself a seducer or intimidator, they will have an adverse effect on the child's psychological development in several ways. The child may be led to believe that he or she is on earth to please others.

Or, the child is made to feel guilty when not pleasing others before self. Worst of all, the intimidation of the young child through harsh or critical language training convinces the child that obedience to authority is the goal of life.

Examples of other words and phrases that the seductive and/or intimidating parental language trainer uses in conversational rape are as follows:

"Say 'May I' or 'Can I' instead of 'I want,' or 'No.'"

Parents often mandate that a child "Be polite and say 'I wish,' or 'Would it be alright,' or 'Could we please do it,' rather than express his or her requests in a straightforward statement of 'I want,' or 'I do not want.'" But couching one's desires in polite or politically correct phrasing actually undermines one's personal worth and self-esteem. The child will grow into an adult who thinks it is unacceptable to express his or her desires without sidestepping into some type of verbal intimidation or seduction to "soften" the request. But the person who can freely say, "I want" and "I do not want," even when it causes others some conflict or pain, is someone who will not be intimidated or seduced into a pattern of conversational rape situations later on in life.

"Tell people you're sorry for your mistakes."

A child who is intimidated or seduced into apologizing for mistakes is really being trained to curtail experimentation. But when exploration and creativity are shut out of the child's personality, the result is stagnation. All potential learning activities are seen to promote mistakes, and the child has been trained to feel guilty about making mistakes. The better way is to assist the child in accepting mistakes as a necessary part of learning in life. The most important lessons we learn in life are the lessons we learn from our mistakes.

"Tell me *why* you think or feel or do things."

Here, the language trainer is saying, in effect, "Prove to me who you are, and only then I will accept you." Since there is no way to prove a *why*, the child eventually loses confidence in both who they are and the validity of their own thoughts and feelings.

Demanding *why* insists the child produce empirical proof, *i.e.* something the questioner can see, taste, touch or hear, which is an impossible burden when dealing with subjective matters. But when you ask a child *What are your reasons?* it only requires the child to provide basic data about a subjective experience, a straightforward statement of feelings or emotions. The parent can then use this as a basis to examine alternative actions resulting from these feelings, and analyze the costs of such actions. Remember, feelings themselves cannot be negotiated, they exist in and of themselves. But you can present an objective *price-prize* case to a child that certain actions taken in response to their subjective feelings have resultant consequences in the world that they should become aware of. They can then learn to make rational choices of how they choose to express natural feelings.

"You *need* me, I am your provider and protector, your trainer."

The child who is taught to "need" certain people, places or things becomes a "needy" adult. All humans have certain basic physiological needs. They need food, water, air and shelter to stay alive. They need strokes or stimulation mentally and physically, either positive pleasure strokes or negative pain strokes, to remain psychologically comfortable. They need a nervous system to record experiences taken in through the five senses of taste, touch, smell, sight and hearing. They need an education to achieve strokes for their mind and body as well as training in how to structure their time on short- and longterm bases. But over-use or misuse of the word —"I *need* to get a new dress," "I *need* a certain person, a certain thing, a certain place to be okay"— is a seduction and/or intimidation of the child into over-emphasis of those people, things, or places. This is conversational rape that undermines their flexible, creative, spontaneous and autonomous way of seeing themselves, others and life in general.

Our Branding in the "OK Corral"

Each one of us holds a basic attitude about life, our *Life Position* which we learned from our language trainers before we were five years old. This is a very subjective view of where we stand in relationship to other people in our lives. Three examples of this attitude reflected in life are as follows:

If we were intimidated by harsh or critical, controlling people, our life position will probably be, "I'm not okay unless I *earn* your conditional love. You are more okay than I am."

Another not-okay position is produced by the over-looking, over-giving, seductive super-parent who seduces the young child into feeling guilty for asserting themselves or contradicting the parent. This child will also carry away a life position of "I'm not okay because I continue to want things," or "Say *no for* me," or "I *should* take care of your needs, not mine." Some churches are also very into promoting this "others first, me second" guilt.

The worst rape of all is the one produced in the drug- or alcoholic-violent home where even a young child knows that the parents are not okay. Out of need and love, however, the child will unconditionally accept a position of, "My parents are not okay and neither am I." This child now has incorporated the type of self-defeating attitude which will later lead to becoming the same type of self-destructor for his or her children.

Gender Differences

Now, let's view a typical situation involving the parents' reaction to a child's level of success in school. It may be politically incorrect to point this out, but there are psychological as well as physical differences between boys and girls. These gender differences necessitate a different parental reaction in each case.

When a little girl brings home a report card and cries that she didn't get all the A's and B's that she thinks everybody wanted her to get, Mommy and Daddy are earnest in providing a balance of *feeling a process*. Daddy would say, "I really do understand you feel bad about your report card, dear, and I think it would be a good idea if you sat down for fifteen minutes every night after supper and went over your math and spelling. How do you feel about this? What can we do to help you feel better? Do you want to stay after school with your teacher? What do you think would be a good system?"

If it's a little boy coming home and crying about the same situation, Mother can say to him, "Son, I do appreciate your situation, but I want to hear what your plans are for improving. And when you know what your plans are, I want you to let us know so that your father and I can assist you in carrying them out." After working out a plan of action together, Mother and Dad can then talk to him about his feelings and nurture him generously.

So in essence, stress is placed on the daughter's feelings, primarily, and then the solution is worked out. With the son, the solution is worked on primarily. Attendance to his feelings is secondary. You cherish a girl's feelings, but respect a boy's abilities to think and problem-solve.

This approach also creates a very good prize because a system is established wherein attention is given to her feelings. She is rewarded, she is stroked, and her performance consequently improves.

To the little boy the parent says, "How do you plan to solve this problem? I want to know what your solution is." The little boy straightens up and says, "Dad, I want to...um...I want you to sit down with me after supper and help me with my school work so I can get better. Will you do that?"

Dad's response is straightforward and reinforces his son's masculinity. "That sounds like a good idea, son."

In each case, you've achieved exactly the same results — to sit down for quiet study after dinner. Then, during the study time, Dad and son can talk about their feelings, whether positive or negative, in order to share and bond.

But, in obtaining these exact same results, what was the principle difference?

With the little girl there was some assistance, some support system underlying reason, but primary attention was given to her feelings; *i.e.,* her sadness, her frustration, her reaction to the bad report card. With the little boy, the feelings were acknowledged, but because he was facing some stress in solving his problem, the parent acted as a coach: "How are you going to solve this, son?" If the boy came up with, "I don't know. I don't know how to solve it," the parents continue with proper encouragement by saying, "Well, we want you to think of a solution and we want you to recognize what that solution is." The boy, importantly, was not discouraged into playing dumb. Rather, he was motivated to solve his problems, and only afterward was consideration for his feelings offered.

On the other hand, the parents first responded to the girl's feelings, then rewarded her, and only when she was feeling better did they assist her in solving her problems.

In families where little girls are raped conversationally and are promoted to act as "little boys," too often the girl will hold her feelings in. As a result, she really can't solve her problems. Suppressing her feelings, she may offer, "I'm going to stay after school," but many times her bad feelings will lead her to decide, "I'm not going to do anything at all." She becomes either rebellious and resistant, or submissive and shy. Very often, a little girl tends either to over-perform in a bid to win objective approval from parents who do not encourage her to share her feelings, or winds up feeling so bad she gives up all such attempts, and under-performs — without sharing her feelings with her parents.

It works exactly the opposite with boys. Little boys very often over-express their feelings. Mommy's boys, initially emotional, receive immediate attention to their feelings, and then somebody even comes in and solves their problems as well. These children eventually grow into young men who learn to employ this process in all their relationships; they yo-yo their feelings in over-use and under-use, manipulating responses from people around them. Little boys who get the idea that the way to solve any problem is to become emotional are in effect learning to use female manipulation tactics. This will not serve them well in the competitive world they will face as grown men.

Similarly, little girls who become so overwhelmed by their feelings, whether over-doing or under-doing in their reactions to their feelings, are facing trouble later on in life. They become an over-do-it parent-mother who gets over-stressed by the demands she places on herself, which negatively affects her health, or morph into a helpless Daisy-Daffodil type of woman, unable to operate without constant human catering. The men in their lives experience them as "high-maintenance" women and very often will ultimately bail out of any relationship, seeing it as too expensive.

Let's conclude by talking for a moment about the parents' role in fostering a child's sexuality.

A significant impact of the report-card scenario we have just discussed is that boys and girls learn not just their self-awareness and self-esteem through language training, but also develop their lifetime sex-role identity. Parents need to be aware of the importance of their cross-gender roles.

Father is more important as a trainer for his daughter than mother is. Father assures his daughter of her sexuality: "You are a woman," or "You are going to be a woman." Mother reinforces the message by telling her, "I'll show you how to do it."

In contrast, Mother assures her son, "You are a boy and you will grow up to be a man, and your Father is going to show you how to do it." And Father will act as the boy's principle male role-model.

Our sexual identity is learned from the opposite-sex parent, but we unconsciously model after the same-sex parent. The confusion a child experiences with either transient, non-existent, or multiple parent figures is therefore easily understood. The confusion is underscored as the child must decide in this early childhood period who which heroes and heroines to identify with.

The significance of language training cannot be over-emphasized. Anyone in a position to provide language training to young children would benefit both themselves and their trainees through exploring therapy programs, including my own program of Androgynous Semantic Realignment,™ WANT® Training.

RESPECT YOUR ELDERS

Conversation

TEENAGER:
>   Do I look good for my date tonight?

DADDY:
>   Get that lipstick off! Do you want people
>   to think you're a bad girl?!?

TEEN-AGER:
>   Please, Dad, all the girls wear it.

DADDY:
>   I don't care. No daughter of mine is going
>   out looking like a tramp.

RAPE!

Rape Analysis

The girl has been conversationally raped of her recognition as a girl in her father's eyes. It is very, very common for fathers who feel significantly threatened by their teen-age daughter's sexuality. They experience guilt about their sexual attachment to their daughter, not realizing this is an absolutely normal occurrence.

As we wrote earlier, the male parent's role is to reassure his daughter of her sexuality, and help her to grow into a properly sexualized woman. Handled well, the natural sexual attachment of a father enhances the girl's self-esteem as a sexual human being.

But if he feels threatened by the daughter's sexuality, the father can fear she will become aware of his response to her and expose him as a "dirty old man." As a result, he will very often discount her feelings as a maturing female, and attack her in matters of clothing and make-up, areas of great significance in the teen years.

If you will recall, the feelings of the body are directly connected to the mind and thinking, and result in action. Little girls are primarily feel–thinkers, while little boys are primarily think–feelers. So when a girl's feelings, especially those she has about her femininity, are attacked or go unsupported, she is significantly castrated as a woman.

Father's discounting daughter's emerging sexuality vis-à-vis her use of lipstick is in effect a rape of that marvelous support which only a father can give as the major male figure in a girl's life.

Ironically, the very fact that the father is attempting to de-emphasize his daughter's sexuality can have the reverse effect of promoting it — but in a negative fashion. Rebellious actions such as sexual promiscuity often result significantly from a female not receiving support as a woman from the leading father figure in her life. She finds extreme difficulty in expressing her femininity appropriately, and will very often become self-destructive. This can find expression in both sexual promiscuity, but also especially and tragically in the areas of over-eating and alcoholism, both of which relate directly to body systems. And sadly, girls not secure about their femininity often sedate their feelings through the use of self-medication and addictive chemicals, *e.g.*, sugar, drugs or alcohol.

So what leads a father to conversationally rape his daughter? It's very likely that he was similarly raped himself earlier in that relationship where his mother figure was significant. A man is threatened by femininity either because of an inappropriate or non-existent relationship with his own mother or the principle female in his life. When he does not feel secure in his own masculinity, his ability to respond is crippled. He cannot hang an identification factor on the male side of his role.

As a consequence, when he becomes a father such a man will not be able to convey masculine support to any female, and this is clearly demonstrated in his relationship with his daughter. Many little girls are Daddy's little girl up to puberty, at which point they are completely abandoned by their fathers. This abrupt rejection has a highly negative effect at a very critical time in their development as maturing women, and impacts their feelings of self-worth as a woman throughout the rest of their lives.

Straight Talk

In talking straight, in terms of a girl and her father, it is helpful to refer to Carl Jung's theory of *anima* and *animus*. which is also demonstrated in the ancient Chinese concept of yin-yang energy balance. Within every female there is her animus element of masculinity, self-assertion and aggressiveness. And within every male there is his anima: his sensitive, intuitive, responsive feminine aspect.

If you will recall my earlier analysis, girls feel–think, with feeling comprising her feminine experience: sensitivity, warmth, responsiveness. If a father does not play the role of "Daddy" by cherishing her exterior feminine (or yin) side then he will instead become a "Father" by generally promoting her interior masculine (or yang) aspect. This results in a woman who cannot cherish her own feelings, a woman who is more into performance than she is into process — in short, an unfeminine woman. And she will have difficulty responding from her female side to any man later in life.

So what can a father do to become more of a "Daddy" and cherish his daughter's feelings? A man cherishes a woman's feelings by maximizing adjective verbiage. He tells her, "You're a *lovely* girl, you're a *loving* person, you're a *kind* person." Adjectives are cherishing statements. Father's use of them promotes daughter's exterior femininity. This allows her to fully feel her interior animus strength internally without sacrificing her femininity externally.

When a woman wears her interior strength on the outside, as a form of protective armor, this costuming as a "man" can only be done at the loss of her feminine exterior. The secret of being a well-balanced woman, starting in her younger years, is to keep her internal strength strictly reserved to herself. To do this, though, she has to feel that her exterior is properly psychologically protected, and this can only be accomplished through the direct cherishing words and actions of a man toward her.

A woman *thinks* in self-preserving terms internally, and gives in a generous way exteriorly. This is exactly opposite to the way a man perceives reality. A man gives in a generous way exteriorly, but *feels* within himself. He still has that female aspect within him called the anima, and when the man takes care of his feelings interiorly, he will generally perform in a self-preserving way.

There is one verbal error that many people make which I call the *Pretty Girl Syndrome*. Prettiness is mistakenly treated as a performance marker: "You look pretty. You dress very well. You do your make-up very well. You keep a good house." But such statements as these are non-adjectives. They are, rather, very performance-oriented strokes.

How can a man change his language into *cherishing* language? He would say, "You're a very *sensuous* woman. You are a very *attractive* woman." These are very nice things to say. A stroked performance is not as fulfilling to a woman as *stroking her process of being a loving woman*.

Basically, a man does better to stroke the magnetic feminine qualities. "You're loving, you're sweet. You're kind and sexy. You're attractive, giving, and you're very generous." Use these statements as opposed to "You *do* something very well."

A male stroke — a performance stroke — would be, "You cook a very good meal."

There is a difference when you say, "That was a very loving thing you did," or "That's a very generous thing you did — the love you show when you cook so well." This is a marvelous statement to make to your daughter.

Now, let's take another look at a possible dialogue between mother and son:

Conversation

SON:
Mom, I'm taking Sally to the Prom.

MOTHER:
No, dear, she's not *our* kind of people.

SON:
But Mom, she's a neat girl and I like her.

DAD:
Listen to your mother, son. She knows best about these things.

RAPE!

Rape Analysis

The first victim is the boy. His choices have been disrespected. Again, one of the primary jobs of mother is to admire and respect her son's brains because that's the part of him that will carry him forward as a man in the world of reality. So mother says in effect, "Son, your brains aren't too cool. Mine are better than yours. I know what's best."

Now, obviously in this case mother has been trained and raised to be a performer herself. She's evaluating the performance level of this "neat girl." Mother's performance orientation begs the question—what happened in her childhood? Likely, there was a father figure or lack of a father figure who promoted the over-stressing of her animus decisional qualities over her instinctive creative qualities. A mother perpetuating a need to be respected for her thinking more than needing to be cherished for her feelings will soon have this young man becoming more and more dependent on her problem-solving capabilities.

He will begin to ask, "Mother, should I? What do you think, Mother?" This will not allow him to identify with the male side of the role and he will eventually become a female-trained man, a second-class operative in society that still prizes the masculine markers of competition, conquering and control.

Dad, on the other hand, is relinquishing his own masculine authority by deferring to a woman's judgement instead of using his own "man-to-man" sharing ability and making his own case toward his son. This indicates that he no doubt deferred to his own mother and other strong women as a young man. Thus, his own rape shows up now in the way he now "trains" his son to similarly defer.

Supporting one another is a good thing for a Mother and Dad, but remaining individuals in their unique masculine and feminine roles is one of the significant gifts they each can give their children.

Straight Talk

How might this situation have been resolved more gender-appropriately? When the son announces, "Mom, I'm taking Sally to the Prom," Mother might have said, "That's nice. What kind of girl is she?" Son would have replied, "She's a great girl, Mom and I like her."

Mom then responds with a positive stroke: "I trust you to use your head, son."

If, on the other hand, Mother sensed something potentially inappropriate was developing, she might have suggested that her son invite this girl over so that she might get to know her.

Mother's feelings are totally appropriate, in that she is being stimulated by her son's emerging sexuality. Once again, Mother and son are having a normal love affair. She is receiving a lot of her masculine strokes from her son, and he is receiving feminine strokes from her. By holding back an immediate expression of her fears and not using them to manipulate the boy's performance or to protect her own feelings, Mother gathers and restructures the situation into one in which she can gather data in her own time and space. She is both taking care of herself and also not castrating her son out of potential fear and inappropriate action.

It's paradoxical. When women use emotion to run their logic, they become illogical. While it's true that women think with their feelings, hopefully they run their feelings through their heads before reacting emotionally.

Men think through their mental logic, but hopefully they apply their logic with a sense of tenderness and sensitive feelings. Since mother is a primary male trainer for her son, it is absolutely appropriate that her vocabulary employ many verbs. "You did that well, son. You're a very bright person. I really *admire* how you did that. I *respect* your choices. I *believe* you know how to do it. Good show, son."

Hopefully, mother and father are the first "love affairs" their children will have. With good sexual communication, the parents will be successful as models for future true affairs.

MAN TO MAN

Conversation

BILL:
> Up for a hot game of racquetball after work?

JOE:
> No, I really haven't played in so long I'd bust something.

BILL:
> Hah, you're just afraid you'll get creamed!

RAPE!

5

Rape Analysis

Bill and Joe are prime examples of what I call Macho/Super Jock and David Daffodil.

Macho-Super Jock Bill is the man who's been raised in a man-centered home, where total emphasis was on his masculine performance capabilities. His feminine process system has been suppressed, described variously as faggy and inappropriate, and he's been indoctrinated that, "Boys don't do that, that's for girls." David Daffodil Joe has obviously grown accustomed to using his feelings over his brains because his brains have been discounted and he cannot trust them for an up-to-snuff performance.

One man has been castrated on the top of the think mountain, and the other has been castrated at the bottom of the feel valley.

Men raised to express themselves exclusively as males, with pressure put on them for performance, respond in one of two ways. Either they over-do and consequently over-act like Macho Bill, or as with Daffodil Joe, they under-do their masculinity and lose faith in themselves. Because neither of these men have their anima feelings under control, they cannot be considered true males. They are both half-men. Their anima feelings have not been incorporated within their thinking, performance, masculine center.

We, in our culture, we admire those who produce more, but what price do we pay for teaching our men to do nothing but perform? What prize do we garner?

The price we pay is that these men become insensitive, they die earlier, and they don't enjoy their lives as much as they could.

There are three levels of stroke systems: people, who are highest quality, nature second, and things third. Naturally, if men are taught that people are not sources of strokes, and that they don't have access to nature, they are not going to till the soil: men are then going to go into their offices for the sole purpose of producing that green stuff called money. Men are going to be encouraged to go out and buy those cars and houses as the only way to express love to the people they care about.

Bill is a man who watches football and other sports as a vicarious "feel" vehicle. Athletics put Bill in touch with other performance males. Athletics afford men such as Bill an opportunity to touch men and feel and perform in a competitive arena.

But for the man who does not allow himself enough time to experience his body, actively watching others is a poor second-best alternative.

For Daffodil Joe, his "over-civilized" castrated *feeling approach* to life may allow him easier access to the feeling world of women. Thus, to earn a living he "joins the women" in feeling-centered occupations, *e.g.*, cosmetology, interior design, fashion or the arts. Even teaching and nursing could be included here.

But the price he pays in over-balance is harsh.

The goal of every human being is balance and integration, which is to say appropriate behavior based on feeling secure internally, thinking logically and acting appropriately.

Bill and Joe are fundamentally out of balance and need assistance in realigning themselves.

You would find, if you tracked Macho Bill long enough, that he will eventually run into the hard wall of reality. Without proper internal balance, Bill will ultimately have his wife run out on him, or he'll lose his job, or he'll get physically sick. Any of these factors will undermine his performance abilities, and he will then go into a depression arising from repressed feelings.

Daffodil Joe is a man straining to perform appropriately, but just not equal to the task. Very often, he acts cowardly or withdraws from reality. He becomes an alcoholic in order to escape his feelings of inadequacy. Or, he becomes a violent man seeking release through intimidating others. He blows up or he blows inward. He is likely to be a latent or an actual homosexual, his true sexuality retreating out of fear of women and their hurtful power.

Straight Talk

Super Jock was raped as a young person in that he was raped of his permission to experience his feelings. It's not necessary to always perform. He can process a feeling as Joe and learn to enjoy the feelings of play as well as the pride in performance. David Daffodil was raped as a young person in that he was not given enough respect for his problem-solving performance ability. As a result, his feelings constantly "swamp" his thinking and consequently he forfeits both his self-esteem and self-worth. He's not only poorly motivated, he's a poor performer.

A more rational back-and-forth about racquetball might go something like this:

BILL:
How about a game of racquetball, Joe?

JOE:
OK, but let me warn you, my game's not really up to par these days.

BILL:
Oh, that's OK, I'm just glad for the game.

JOE:
Thanks, and I'll do my best and give you a run for your money.

Now, the two men are more human, seeking the goals of balance, integration and appropriate behavior based on feeling secure internally, thinking logically and acting appropriately.

WOMAN TO WOMAN

Conversation

ALICE:

> You really should get your hair colored, Mary.
> It would make you look years younger.

MARY:

> Do you really think so, Alice? I don't know
> anything about such things.

ALICE:

> I'll make an appointment with my hairdresser,
> dear. We're going to get you all fixed up.

RAPE!

6

Rape Analysis

Once again both people have been raped, either currently or in the past. But in this particular case, the rape is more subtle.

Being women, both of these ladies are given to feeling statements. Alice portrays in her exhibition of language what I call Super-Mom Bertha Balls. Simply stated, she's doing the active giving for and to another person in order to exercise control. She is a lady who was taught, probably by a father who was performance-oriented and by a mother who did perform as Super or Critical Mom, or didn't perform at all, choosing the role or Daisy Daffodil. One of these extremes encouraged Alice into performing. As a result, she's determined to rescue poor little Mary who doesn't know how to fix her hair. She is, in effect, over-extending herself.

Mary, on the other hand, is playing stupid Daisy Daffodil. By being stupid, Mary can seduce Alice into rescuing her. Alice invited action on the part of Mary, and perpetuates Mary's self-recognized powerful passivity. I make the statement here, which may sound incongruous but is nonetheless true, that the passive person is the one in control in this situation, the powerful one, and that the person who is in the active role is generally the more helpless. Alice is being raped at this time because she is in effect being seduced into doing a performance to take care of Mary. Mary has been raped in the past, and is now in the process of raping Alice. Mary does this by being the helpless, inactive, but passively powerful woman.

Straight Talk

Women are predominantly process-oriented, feeling-centered, body-centered human beings who use their brains to take care of their feelings, their bodies, and their processes. So let's examine the dialogue between two healthy, individuated women.

The dialogue for this situation would first have Alice *requesting Mary's permission* to make a suggestion about her appearance. When Mary gives her a go-ahead, Alice's comment to Mary might be, "I suggest that you think about having your hair colored. Are you willing to do that?" Mary would then respond, "I appreciate your caring about my hair. I want to think about that before I take action. I appreciate your caring about my looks."

Let's spend some time examining the roles of women in today's society. It is my opinion that we are at the apex if an emergence of a new entity for women and their process/performance integration.

In the past, our concern has been directed toward woman's performance in the home, and had traditionally discounted women's capabilities in performing in the "Man's World" of, for example, banking, sales, construction and top executive strategizing. We gave women permission to perform in "feminine occupations" like nursing and teaching, but not to operate in spheres like engineering and other traditional male bastions.

Today, thanks to the Women's Lib movement, which is basically an economic shift more than an psychological movement, we have seen women move into many if not most occupations formerly dominated by men. Women have gained more legal, business, professional and economic privileges and are now pretty much on an equal footing with men when it comes to earning a living. And this is a good thing, for both women and men. There is a firm sense of equality in the workplace.

There have come to light, however, unintended consequences of this paradigm shift in our society. One of these consequences is a psychological problem, that of extremism. There are career women who are performance-oriented. These Bertha Balls and Super Moms have begun to face-off with more traditional housewives who are process-oriented Daisy Daffodils, and each camp has become highly critical of the other.

To be sure, there are women who are becoming too performance-oriented. They are losing the female priority system and not concentrating on process. The typical "Women's Libber," with all the inappropriate aggressive manifestations, is really a woman hater. She has voluntarily entered into competition with men for work in a man's world, competing with both men and other women in a male world for a male position and the prize of economic independence. But the psychological costs of this competition have become greater liabilities than the financial gain and the achievement of economic equality.

On the other hand, Daisy Daffodil may be choosing to over-react by absenting herself from all competition by staying home. Daisy has elected not to test her abilities in the marketplace, responding to a feeling of repulsion at the harshness of the "Woman's Libber." Sadly, Daisy pays her own price in staying under-developed as a woman.

The appropriately blended woman is one who predominantly knows what she wants based on her own unique sensitivity, and then goes after it. She does not allow herself to be stampeded into competitive performance based on somebody else's direction. She does not allow herself to be intimidated into leaving her home if she does not want to leave it. The appropriately blended woman can be as good a woman at home as she can be in an office.

Too many times, home-oriented women are being discounted and intimidated into leaving their homes based on their Woman's Lib sister accusing them of not being progressive women. But staying home, and performing at home, may be exactly what the home-oriented woman wants. Some women who are "out there" and pushing for performance are going at it in such an insensitive, controversial, and antagonistic way that they're creating bad feelings not only in business and society but also among home-oriented okay women.

Women in today's world would do well to continue to process their own feelings, whatever they may be. Good use of their brain would be in channeling those feelings. My want is to give women permission to perform rationally, logically, and to see themselves as good women, anywhere they work, inside or outside the home.

In times now long past, women were seen as "the other half of their men." Men went out to work and earn the money to provide for the nest. Women stayed at home and created a stable environment in which to raise a brood. They were called homemakers (and not "housewives"), a description of their chosen occupation. With the migration of women into business and industry during the Second World War, a conflict has arisen in the old half-and-half system. Women became aware of the fact that they, too, could do well "out there" and with this awareness came a new choice.

As women have gathered more economic power through ERA-type legislation and NOW (National Organization of Women), they have begun campaigning to "free the slaves" still at home. And just as our country exhibited confusion over Abraham

Lincoln's freeing the slaves after the Civil War and more recently the consequential racial problems of the Sixties, we experienced woman's issues problems in the Seventies and Eighties.

Today it has become even more complicated, as we have an entire generation of women who were raised by mothers who came into their own during those turbulent times. These young ladies have only one role model on which they can base their sexuality: the "libber." They have no freedom to accept or reject the more traditional woman's role, because they have no direct experience of witnessing it in their lives. Unless they are into reading historical novels or studying psychological examinations of past generations, they have only a single concept of total equality with men, process-oriented lives, and the unavoidable and destructive stress that comes from competing in a man's game, both in the boardroom and in the bedroom, with tools that were never designed for such competition — namely, their feelings.

As I have pointed out before, women tend to be feeling-centered performers as opposed to men, who are thinking-centered processors. Women today are face-to-face with a major problem, and the only solution, as I see it, is getting a clear idea of what the term "performance" means, for a man and for a woman.

Being a business or industry performer is neither more nor less valuable than a homemaker who runs a first-rate home. The basic cognitive and physical skills are still used in both areas. The only real difference is in the amount and way money is exchanged for the performance.

The businesswoman earns a salary from the company she works for. The homemaker earns her salary from the man she works for.

This may appear to be "degradation" and "dependence" to many independent-minded women. It has been recognized in the top business circles, however, that "A man at the top must have a woman at the top at home to be any good." A good man needs to have a well-run home as part of his support structure. He needs the security of a stable home environment in order to recharge his batteries from the stress of competing in the workplace. As I have said earlier, man has within himself all the anima sensitivity and vulnerability and creativity that women have. This anima must have a place to emerge from the protective shell of masculine competency it hides in during the workday, and a safe, attractive, well-run home is the ideal environment. It can make him a truly fit and blended man.

The top-drawer homemaker is the "man" at home behind the man in business. By her homemaking efforts, she deserves half the credit and half the money for his success. In effect, she has earned her pay for the day when she has created an environment where her man can relax and be his authentic self for a time.

It is pure hyperbole on the part of the Woman's Lib movement when they protest that women are still being dominated, used and abused by men. A woman who elects to stay at home is not being dominated. She is being preceded by a man who sees and acknowledges all her efforts behind his leadership, as both a protector and a supporter. As he leads her into a successful lifestyle, he protects and provides — and as she follows him, she supports and comforts him. Together, they become a successful team.

When women see themselves in competition at home with their men, confusion reigns — the man is not allowed to lead, assert, protect, provide and his partner does not respond, follow, or offer support. The scenario is one of all chiefs and no indians. The lamentable result of this competition for "Chief" equality is that no one wins.

On the other hand, some women who do emerge as "liberated" into the business arena do so with the anticipation that being equal to a man is *the good* and that happiness will somehow result from equality. The dismal dawning is that, this equality brings as much stress and heartache as happiness, fosters blandness, and leads to unclear gender roles, particularly in the social arena.

As a result, in areas both business and personal, men and women are becoming more and more confused about proper and fulfilling ways to relate to each other. Role reversals and conflicting sex role identities have become a way of life in the 21st Century.

My premise is that all is equal and fair in *performance-centered business*. My own highly successful career as a woman therapist in what was originally a man's professional domain has borne this out, and enabled me to use my gifts and talents and abilities to help thousands of individuals and couples find true individuation and fulfilling emotional and sexual relationships.

But, in those *process-centered personal and sexual areas*, women and men are differentiated in a number of physiological and psychological areas, and those core differences demand awareness and respect if we are to have successful interpersonal relationships.

The blended man tends to feel and process his way through life better when he is encouraged and supported in his assertion, leadership, teaching, protecting, providing, and active giving roles. The blended woman, similarly, tends to feel and perform better when she is encouraged and allowed to respond to her man's sensitive leadership in a protected environment. In the ideal male-female relationship, her man seeks out and cherishes her feelings in a loving, giving way. Actively, she responds to him our of respect for his skills in thinking and doing. And since she is in the power-position, it is tantamount on the part of the woman to initiate the flow of energy, by first respecting the man she has chosen to pledge her life to.

In sum, an authentic, smart woman respects her man's brains while an authentic, smart man then cherishes his woman's feelings. Together, they negotiate to design a life which may include the woman either staying at home or going to work. Whatever the decision, they remember to honor their unique individual priorities as a man and a woman in their personal relationship.

So, women have a new cultural problem— accepting and managing the diversity of priorities between career and home orientation. These new choices also affect their relationships with their men. Resolving both of these challenges in a mutually satisfying solution seems to be a central issue of today's world.

SWEET TALK

Conversation:

BILL:
> I'm going to take you out this weekend and show you what a really good time is...Haha!

MARY:
> But, Bill, I already have a date.

BILL:
> Break it!

MARY:
> Okay, Bill. I'll do it for you.

RAPE!

Rape Analysis

Bill exhibits the type of performance-oriented behavior common to Macho-Super Jocks. He is dominating, intimidating, insensitive, pushy, grabby — any and all terms of this nature. In effect, however, Bill is probably very frightened and his strategy to deal with these feelings is by over-compensating. Therefore, he steamrollers Mary. She is allowing herself to be conversationally raped into a Daisy Daffodil passive position because now she can say, "It's not my fault, he raped me."

Mary feigns helplessness when she says, "But Bill, but Bill," and Bill overrides her protests, giving Mary the excuse of having been socially raped because he is so pushy. In the eventual long-run scheme, however, Bill is the one who would be raped because he would be responsible for Mary and her rape, and the rape of the guy she was supposed to date in the first place. In blaming the whole situation on Bill, Mary can collect her angry stamps, and continue her games with other men.

Straight Talk

Were this invitation effectively restated, Bill and Mary could conceivably talk as follows:

Rational Conversation:

BILL:
> Mary, I want to take you out this weekend if you're available.

MARY:
> I appreciate your invitation. But the fact is, I already have a date. Are you willing to ask me again?

BILL:
> Sure.

In the case of women relating to each other, and men, some women control with passivity. As pointed out earlier, it is significant and important in an intimate relationship for a woman to respect a man. Since Bill has taken the risk of pursuing or reaching out to Mary, she has a choice. She can be helpless and passive or she can be active, self-controlled, and responsible for herself. The latter choice disallows games.

By her sensitive responsiveness and consideration for his feelings, Mary rejects the invitation respectfully, promoting a willingness on Bill's part to reach out to her as a woman in the future.

Macho Super-Jock Bill tends to be very attractive to Daisy Daffodil Mary, in that Daisy is totally in charge of feelings, and Super-Jock is totally in charge of thinking. Between the two of them, they become one whole person. On the reverse side, Bertha Balls, the very performance-oriented woman, is very attracted to David Daffodil, a very passive-character man, in the same way that Macho and Daisy are attracted. Relationships are based either on rational systems or emotional systems. If they're based on rational systems then the man and woman complement, but do not replace, each other. In that way, the man brings a performance–process system and woman brings a process–performance system into the relationship. Both have permission to feel. He and she each have a separate responsibility to see that their particular side of the fence is in good repair. The man is in charge of problem-solving and the woman is in charge of the feeling level. In this way, no performance is done which may cause her significant pain and eventually reflect negatively on his performance.

Here is another sweet-talk exchange:

Conversation:

ALICE: (On their third date)
...And Joe, it's okay if you spend the night rather than drive home.

JOE:
Sounds nice, Alice, but where do I sleep?

ALICE:
Wherever you want.

RAPE!

Rape Analysis:

Alice is a pursuer, a performance-oriented female. She needed stroking and has opted to use the male system of dynamic pursuit over the female system of magnetic attraction to obtain those strokes. In her undercover message, which she has conveyed at the lower game level, she is inviting Joe to play with her sexually. Many women allow the intimacy of intercourse when what they really want are strokes of friendly affection — TLC. One of the big promotional abuses in the world today is telling women that they can experience intimate intercourse indiscriminately without hurting themselves. Since women are feel–thinkers and need to be safe and trusting for true sexual surrender, a woman who either invites or allows fast sex runs the risk of desensitizing herself to a total orgasmic experience.

In this dialogue, Bertha Balls Alice is herself being raped of her rights to be a woman. She's not allowing herself to be sensitive, to move slowly, to be courted and pursued by a risk-taking male who knows how to solve problems, knows what he wants and goes after it. And our friend, passive David Daffodil Joe is now in the magnificent *power* position of receiving all of this deep generosity promoted by Bertha. Sadly, Bertha is really promoting Daffodil Joe's passivity. Also, Joe's negative attitude for women, as objects, things to use and play with, is being promoted.

Straight Talk

It is my experience that men want to solve problems so that they can feel very, very self-reliant. They want to feel in charge, in control, and responsible when they do the performance pursuing. When Joe is pursued, he does not go through the process of problem solving. Therefore, he is actually at the mercy of Alice, which in effect undermines his masculinity and promotes his negativity. Because he feels this lack of control, he subconsciously distrusts her and will, in effect, use her, abuse her, and then ultimately leave her for another woman.

In this new choice, Joe will feel comfortable entrusting his feelings to a woman who loves herself more than Alice does, who he can consider a worthy trustee of his own love feelings. Falling in love takes time, and effort, but the value is more enduring.

Relationships are constructed on two different systems. One system is very definitely protective, the friendship foundation system. It protects the sensitivities of both parties and also allows the rational experience of the two elements of compatibility and communication.

The other system is based on chemical communication between two sensuous people who are more interested in "thing" body strokes than in spiritual love, sharing and care strokes. As long as both people want the same thing, they will be okay. The risk comes when one wants love strokes and the other wants lust.

People often go to bed in order to *eliminate intimacy*, because true intimacy carries risk-taking pain. The massive modern fascination with sexual-chemistry relationships places compatible communication second. Relationships based on friendship place compatibility and communication first, and chemistry second. Eventually, if the chemistry is there, the inherent negotiation of compatibility and communication will allow the sexual experience in a safe, loving way.

In consideration of the male, all too often today's man is being promoted to perform sexually. They are ending up with all kinds of sexual dysfunction that they've never had before. As I said before, when a man solves his problems, he feels more potent and he's correspondingly more sexually potent as well. He is in charge of the situation and when he's in charge of the situation and behavior, then the female part of him feels safe. When a man pursues a woman and he pursues her by being a trustworthy, honorable person then he can, in effect, relax and enjoy himself.

A man who has been seduced and manipulated by his woman into thinking he's responsible for giving her orgasms, however, is a raped man. His problem will be manifested variably, from premature ejaculation to seminal retention, to impotence. The job is not performed because he knows subconsciously he shouldn't perform it. The accomplishment is not good for him as a man. Don't blame yourself because you didn't get the job done.

For example, in terms of the premature ejaculator, you're saying that you had better get your compatibility, friendship and love factors lined up because the chemistry is being damaged.

Seminal retainers are hanging on. You're really saying that you don't want to surrender. You don't want to give because there is something inappropriate about the person you are with or, it may be that you have still not resolved about your fear of demanding, taking women. Psychologically, the easiest understood sexual dysfunction is impotence. Impotence is saying, "I won't do it. And you can't make me do it, lady."

Men, since they are very much interested in performance, are in charge of the concrete world. They see a pretty body, they want to touch it. That is very concrete. Women, on the other hand, are in charge of the abstract, spiritual world, and they, in fact, are very much into not being touched unless they feel safe.

So, when a man sees a pretty girl he responds to her concretely. When a woman sees a man, she thinks about his likability, his lovability. When two needy people relate we say they are symbiotic, parasitic. They need each other to fulfill themselves. Healthy people want each other but do not need. I say that people come in two varieties; one shouldering the question "Who am I?" and the other directly an "I," *i.e.*, "I am myself and I know who I am."

Symbiotic people simply do not share. They, give, they take— but they do not share. One is a giver and the other a taker. In a sharing relationship, there is also give and take. Additionally they also ask for and refuse from time to time. Importantly, however, in a sharing relationship each individual predominantly takes care of themselves first.

Independent people are internally secure. Their childhoods were stable and they now feel well-loved by people. When they seek intimacy, they do so with the capacity to share that love with other people. The person who is not internally secure is anxious, constantly looking for love and a safe environment. When they find what they think they are looking for, they latch on, creating a mutually needy dependent relationship. Both lose, as both people continue to promote a lack of independence or "I" centeredness.

Rational Conversation:

ALICE:

>Joe, I enjoyed our date tonight, and I don't want to feel afraid for your safety. Will you be careful when you drive home?

JOE:

>It was nice, Alice, and I'll be careful. When can I see you again?

'TIL DEATH DO US PART

<u>Conversation:</u>

BILL or ALICE:
    Why don't you _____?

JOE or MARY:
    I can't because _____.

RAPE!

Rape Analysis

Again, we are viewing Super-Jock Macho Bill, Bertha Balls Alice, and their counterparts — David Daffodil and Daisy Daffodil Mary. All are intent on conversationally raping each other, just like Mom and Dad did to them when they were little.

Macho Bill and Bertha Balls Alice believe that action is more powerful than inaction, but they are mistaken. Daffodil Mary and Daffodil Joe can side-step with their helpless, passive aggressive games until Bertha and Macho are themselves victims of both frustration and resentment.

When Macho and Bertha finally catch on to the rape and stop trying to get control of the relationship through power plays, they find that their Daffodil opposites take up the game and begin pressuring them in a role reversal. People who use active power are actually more afraid than the "powerless" passive partner who is safe enough to sit back and watch the fireworks. Remember, it is the one-down victim who actually gets the strokes from others — sympathy, pity, empathy, and rescuing. Bertha and Macho usually get left alone, looked down on, undermined in this scenario as the "B-movie" bad guys.

Marriage or committed one-to-one relationships built on a one-up, one-down system contain two question mark people. They are two humans, each of whom needs to trigger a rape in order to get a painful reaction like they remember from home.

Symbiotic, parasitic marriages can function indefinitely as long as no one moves out of line. If Bertha or Macho break down or Daisy or David build up, then a domino effect takes place which influences the whole family, including relatives who do not live with them. This can be a very good thing in a marriage, but often it ignites escape mechanisms like over-eating, excess drinking, or extra-marital non-negotiated affairs. If the changing people are open and honest, they can adjust to the new equality of "I'm okay and so are you." Professional help may be needed during this transition.

Straight Talk

In a good, balanced relationship, both people exhibit all varieties of behavior appropriately in response to all types of behavior in their partner. If a man cherishes his woman's feelings, he will listen to her without judgement and support her not-wants and general wants as much as he can, as long as they are moral, ethical and legal. If a woman respects her man's thinking, she will listen to his specific wants and not-wants and respond to them as much as she can, as long as they are moral, ethical and legal. Together they complement each other and individually they grow and prosper. As they become more "I"-centered, they have more to share as a "we" couple and as an "us" couple in society.

This free exchange regarding individual wants and not-wants is handled by verbal negotiation.

In any committed relationship, there are four areas of negotiation — time, space, play (non-sexual and sexual) and money.

The first area of negotiation, time, comprises three subdivisions: time together as a "we," time alone as an "I," and time as a couple in relation to other persons as "us." Healthy individuals make certain that they negotiate all three categories appropriately, *i.e.*, I, we, and us. They maintain a balance among the three areas, being careful to avoid gamey "rape" deals wherein they intimidate or seduce each other out of balance.

Symbiotic couples over-depend on each other as a "we." Their alone time as well as their socializing with outsiders is reduced as they exhibit a pathetic need to hang on to each other just as they did with mommy and daddy before they were five years old.

Individuals who are still fixated at an early level of growth usually believe that with good performance they can earn love.

The contrary is true: you can never earn love conditionally.

By its very nature, true love is unconditional and only mature "I"-centered individuals can truly share it by accepting each other, as is, and being willing to negotiate without resorting to the tactics of intimidation or seduction.

The second area of negotiation is personal space, how it is shared and how it is cared for. We live in a possessive-pronoun world — my closet, your drawer, our dishes, my chores, your chores. One of the first words a child learns is "mine" and we carry the concept of ownership into adulthood with amazing tenacity. Too often symbiotic couples wrongly believe everything belongs to "we" and then a rape situation occurs in which private ownership and a blurring of responsibilities takes place, which only promotes games and brings both pain and a breakdown of intimacy. To know where lines have been drawn is to establish stability, forestall misunderstandings and promote closeness.

The third and fourth areas of negotiation are sex and money, respectively. Their inherent lines of responsibility draw perimeters around our two biggest areas of conversational rape.

Few couples have only physical sex problems. Most sex dysfunction is based on communication difficulties. Symbiotic, needy, question-mark people usually attempt to intimidate or seduce each other into a possessive, obsessive relationship. They disallow any space between them for such things as friendships with the opposite sex or a social life with same-sex friends. They very often become more needy and dependent since no one person can fully satisfy the stroke hunger in another person.

A well-negotiated couple, on the other hand, allows for social interaction, even flirting—as long as it's kept within clearly couple-established guidelines. These include sexual exclusivity, and the knowledge that a comfortable, free person will feel more inclined to respond to an accepting, non-demanding partner than a punitive, controlling partner.

In the area of money, the power rape games come out in full force. Money has a spiritual power even greater than that of sex. Whoever controls the purse strings controls the relationship's health. The most balanced negotiation is to create clearly defined categories of "my money," "your money," and "our money."

In this system, even when there is only one income, a portion is given to the non-paid partner to do as they please. It is disastrous for one or the other of the couple to "ask for" pin money. It automatically establishes a conversational rape situation. One person may be the designated bookkeeper: he or she may write the checks, keep the business details straight, and balance the budget, but that person benefits more by sharing the decision responsibilities with the other.

In earlier chapters, I have talked about dealing with children appropriately. In this chapter on marriage, I want to summarize a statement about children relative to the four areas of couple negotiation — time, space, sex, and money. In these areas, children can share the negotiation during family council time (talking). But remember, the primary responsibility for setting up a good communication system is between husband and wife. Any time children outrank a husband or wife, trouble occurs. A man and a woman may not totally agree with each other but they negotiate between themselves about the rules of the house — the do's and the don'ts, the wants and not wants — before bringing the children into the transaction. When they arrive at a good negotiated compromise, they support each other in front of the kids in order to establish secure stable guidelines for the marriage and for the family.

The purpose in all this negotiation is to establish clearly defined guidelines for the direction and goals of the relationship. In the absence of preplanning, the only alternative is spontaneous decision-making. And total spontaneity invites chaos.

In contrast, self-discipline makes room for occasional spontaneous activity, by creating an atmosphere of knowledgeable security in which it is safe to experiment. Both adults and children feel safer knowing where they stand in relationship to each other. With continuing open conversations, any couple can maintain a flowing, free, fun relationship. They can teach their children by example to avoid power games of intimidation or seduction. And they can teach their children to avoid the conversational rape of others.

OFFICE POLITICS

<u>Conversation:</u>

SUPERVISOR:
    No excuses — just get it done today!

CLERK:
    But I can't get it all done today because —

SUPERVISOR:
    Well, if you can't do your job we'll get
    someone else around here who can.

RAPE!

Rape Analysis

People in authority have power, but sometimes the exercise of their power indicates a lack of personal potency within themselves. Careers and jobs which stress one-up boss and one-down employee often attract needy, question-mark people. Legal careers, careers in law enforcement, the military, medicine, politics...these are the most obvious places where this happens. But more subtle, power-sensitive careers in teaching, the ministry, and the junior/senior executive ladder in business also promote one-upmanship. Needy people, out of fear of not trusting themselves, focus more on survival rather than on success. They often promote and invite domination, using conversational rape of mendicancy. Their talk is always "May I, please?" or "Would it be alright?" instead of "I want — may I?"

On the other hand, there are boss persons who cover their insecurity with shows of domination: "You should do it my way or else!" With these tactics, they are indicating that they do not believe in their ability to successfully negotiate their wants. They decide instead to use a power play. Ironically, such a power-centered person often goes home to become a powerless pawn in their husband or wife relationship, a Daisy or David Daffodil.

This is especially prevalent in the "god" professions. Doctors, lawyers, ministers, therapists and teachers can easily take advantage of the ignorance and fear in their patients, clients, and students. When their actions promote insecurity, they are perpetuating the rape system in society in a significant way as these high-profile careers symbolically duplicate the parental roles which launched the individual's identity system in the first place.

Straight Talk

On the positive side of this coin, these "parental" careers have the great potential to do much to promote "I"-centeredness and emotional stability in the persons they deal with throughout their careers, because these professions do represent current parental messages, properly tailored to replace prior negative communication in the lives of their patients clients and employees.

Such a positive office request might be as follows:

Rational Conversation

SUPERVISOR:
I want this job done today. Will you do it?

CLERK:
I want to do it today, and I will unless something interferes. I'll let you know by 2 o'clock this afternoon if I am not able to get it done.

SUPERVISOR:
Fine, if you need some help, ask.

In this dialogue, the same request was made, but in a more

potent and healthier way for both parties.

THROUGH THICK AND THIN

Conversation

SUPERMOM:
> Oh, come on. One more drink (or helping)
> won't hurt you.

VICTIM:
> You're right, I guess one more drink (or
> helping) won't hurt me. Haha!

RAPE!

10

Rape Analysis

For the man, woman or child with poor self-esteem, food, drink and drugs are a way to give themselves "thing" strokes to replace the people strokes they fear. We all need stroke stimulation, either positive or negative, and we also need to structure our time to obtain strokes.

Strokes come in three varieties. The highest quality strokes are those which can bring the greatest pleasure or pain, and they come from people — especially those with whom we are intimate. The second level of strokes comes from nature: animals, plants, the sky, sand, grass, and the outdoors in general. Many people use outdoor nature strokes to maintain a major portion of their stroke ecology. They structure their time to include walking, jogging, running, swimming, gardening and many other forms of outdoor exercise.

The lowest quality stroke comes from "things." These replace human interaction, and include any impulsive compulsive activity like food, drink, drugs, money, or sex for sex's sake. Children who learn too early that their world is filled with pain due to a poor family relationship often turn to things to fill their world in a safer way. This bad habit grows with them into adulthood, leaving them unskilled in communicating wants and not-wants. They exist only as victims. They have been conversationally raped.

Pain-filled homes produce two kinds of children. There are those who believe that pain is the normal state of existence and pleasure should be avoided. Others believe pain will kill them and must be sedated with alcohol, sugar, or drugs. I call them the pain addict and the non-pain addict. They very often marry each other later in life in order to maintain emotional balance.

The pain addict victim will discount compliments. This person will stay in jobs, marriages, and relationships of negative quality. They generally see only the dark side on all occasions. They are not pleasant people to be around.

The no-pain addict may seem cheerful when all is going well, or while they are sedated with chemicals. At the first sign of anxiety or pain, however, they panic and run for emotional cover. Thus, they never learn how to protect themselves from rape conversation.

Straight Talk

Both the pain and the no-pain addict need to be re-educated in how to get the higher quality stroke from humans. They need to be taught how to communicate their wants and not-wants verbally, in a rational, free manner. Very often they must be taught that pain is a symptom, not a disease. It is an indication that change is needed or change is in progress. Pain will never destroy them or anyone else.

In order to become fully functioning adults, these persons must learn the lesson that unless we each are willing to give and take pain, we may never learn how to take care of ourselves or relate to one another. We each can hurt ourselves through mismanagement of pain, but it is our responsibility, not "theirs," if we do so.

By learning to talk straight, and express our wants and not-wants without resorting to trickery, intimidation, guilt or subtle gamesmanship, we learn to channel our normal negative feelings into positive energy. Anger, guilt, sadness, resentment, or frustration, for example, that flow through our sober thinking can motivate us to act rationally and productively.

No healthy person wishes to sustain a negative feeling. As we grow into fully actualized human beings, we realize a profound truth:

The healthy way to overcome a negative feeling is to make a positive decision, followed by action (or a cessation of negative action) in support of that decision.

There are two main motivational mechanisms in our lives: pain, which drives us away from those things we do not want, and pleasure, which draws us toward those things that we do want. A good combination of human, nature, and thing strokes lends itself to a balanced life based not on pain, but on pleasure.

OLD FOGIES

<u>Conversation:</u>

GRANDMA/GRANDPA:
>   We'll baby-sit for you, honey.

SON/DAUGHTER:
>   No, Mom and Dad, you just sit right down and enjoy your retirement...you've earned it.

GRANDMA/GRANDPA (unspoken):
>   But we don't want to sit around waiting to die. We want to be a part of the family.

RAPE!

11

Rape Analysis

And so it is at the end of our lives in this country. By promoting dependency on the young or the government, we often condemn our senior citizens to a sentence of both sitting idle and waiting for death.

It can often appear as if we force elderly people back into filial symbiosis reminiscent of the original infant symbiosis. Once again, language and conversation can happily perpetuate autonomy, creativity and spontaneity. Or, language can insidiously perpetuate rape through power play conversations.

In families where only the "useful" money makers participate in family decision making, senior citizens lose the vote. They lose their voice when they lose their earning power. They are seen in human function as no more then babysitting sources or immediately available money lenders, with no questions asked.

Sometimes the elderly are convinced to sell homes they love and move into ghetto retirement villages. Some, *but certainly not all*, of these retirement centers equate with pre-school childcare establishments. Those that are poorly designed limit movement under a watchful eye; in a disguise of entertainment, institutional care is pushed.

Sometimes, when chronic medical problems exist which interfere with the social life of the family, Mom and Dad become a burden to be suffered from a distance. Medical and behavioral sciences talk about the need for body contact and intimacy for the young child. Ironically, the elderly person with the same problems is often neglected.

Possessive children sometimes refuse to support or encourage budding romances among the elderly. These children do so out of misguided visions of senior citizens as sexless; people not in need of either relationships or the intimacy they can provide. Companionship at this time of life is an actual aid to longer life. In point of fact, mutual caring and sharing with another human being promotes physical, mental, and emotional health.

On the other side of the fence, there are elderly persons who take advantage of their "second childhood" and often revert to behavior classified as "spoiled" in children. Verbal demands, whines for attention, and willful, rejecting actions will surely promote conversational rape for all parties. The guilty or angry younger person resents being taken advantage of by the willful parent, and often retaliates by rejecting and abandoning the parent in their twilight years.

Also, there is the phenomenon of the "helpless" Daisy and David Daffodil elderly couple, which can totally disrupt the family life of a child by refusing to promote self-centered care and responsibility. It almost appears that the parents are seeking a "payback" for all the services rendered to the dependent son or daughter years earlier.

Straight Talk

In an appropriate and healthy relationship between senior and junior family members, there exists a conversational system which is founded on "I want" and "I do not want." Rape does not exist because respect permeates the relationship. Whenever possible, situations which occur are negotiated on equal terms. No one is one-up or one-down due to physical or mental standing. Love has become the watchword.

Children raised by rational, child-centered couples later become rational, loving parents to the couple who raised them. They end the cycle of life on the same theme — feelings and not-wants are to be cherished, and thoughts and wants are to be respected, by using the mind to design loving actions which promote self-love, respect and esteem.

The purpose of life is to have the experience of living. The experience of living, in turn, is to seek pleasure and love for self and to share it with others. The only behavior that is totally learned, totally environmental, is the behavior of love. This is in contrast to given hereditary characteristics in the physical, mental and emotional areas. We learn to love ourselves from our parents through language. We share this with others the same way.

When parents teach children to love themselves successfully, they are almost certain to guarantee a comfortable old age in which this loving lesson returns tenfold in loving concern and respect.

TO THINE OWN SELF
BE TRUE

<u>Conversation</u>

INTERNAL CRITICAL PARENT:
You should have done it better, stupid.

ADAPTED CHILD-SELF:
You're right, I should have done it better.
I *am* stupid.

RAPE!

12

Rape Analysis

As I have said in the early chapters dealing with the conversational rape of children under five, poor language training leads to an inhibition of the child's autonomy, creativity, and spontaneity.

Parents, schools, churches, and cultures often teach children, for example, that mistakes are wrong, or you must know before you do something that it is right, good and proper or don't risk doing it.

Such teachings are in error. You and I can be autonomous only if we believe that we will not be rejected or abandoned by those we love because we did something wrong.

Conditional love crushes creativity or spontaneity because it mandates that we must follow "shoulds" that others deem appropriate, rather than wants which we intuitively seek out of pleasure for ourselves.

Straight Talk

Once again, I'm going to make what will at first seem like a politically incorrect statement. But follow through on my logic.

Emotionally healthy people are self-centered people. Self-centered people often seem selfish, impolite, foolish, crazy, immoral or downright illegal, because they are completely willing to follow their own inner spirit and to risk making mistakes. People who are selfless, however, are inherently unhealthy. Selfless people often seem generous, polite, logical, moral and legal — but it's because they compromise their integrity to fit themselves to the design of their surroundings. They do this by sacrificing their personal wants, and embracing the security of the *shoulds* imposed on them from the outside by family, friends and society in general.

From these propositions, we see that people come in two styles. They are either "I"-centered or they are question-mark (?) people.

"I"-centered people reason within themselves about the prices and prizes of possible actions. They do or do not do things depending upon what they personally will get out of an action they take. They never give or take things from other people over five years old unless they personally will benefit. By personally profiting from an action, they unconditionally accept or reject their gift. They have already received their internal prize of personal pleasure, self-esteem, self-love and self-respect.

Question-mark (?) people always do things for or against others because they react to shoulds from outside themselves. If they do something for someone, they assume and expect a reward. They have an overriding motto emblazoned across their coat of arms: "I do this for you, therefore you should pay me back." Their lives comprise an unending tally sheet, wherein they constantly check to see if they are in the black or in the red. And since they are usually in the red, they are constantly angry because other people are perceived as not properly paying them back for all the generous gifts they have freely bestowed upon their vassals, without request.

Inside every generous "Super Parent" person hides a sad little "Adapted Child," who was taught before age five that *shoulds* were better than *wants* as a medium through which to earn love and avoid rejection and abandonment.

Inside every intimidating "Critical Parent" person hides an angry, rebellious little "Adapted Child" who learned before age five that people are just plain mean and hurtful. They learned that the only way to avoid the pain of rejection and abandonment was to "get them before they get you."

Inside every "Nurturing Parent" person is a happy, curious, mischievous, brave little "Fun Free" child who goes after what he or she wants. And they spontaneously pull away from what they don't want, because they learned before age five that love is never earned by good behavior. They learned that love is given freely because we exist in a world of sharing, caring people who themselves have learned that love is free.

When we talk to ourselves, we have two choices.

We can harass, criticize, dominate, intimidate and conversationally rape ourselves like "they" taught us when we were little.

Or, we can love ourselves unconditionally and share that love with others. We can nurture and accept ourselves and others, even when we make mistakes or they make mistakes.

I don't need to like or approve of other people.

I do need to love and accept or reject them but not tolerate them.

By talking straight to ourselves and others, we demonstrate unconditional loving acceptance and pleasure results.

A sample, more loving dialogue, follows:

Rational Conversation

NURTURING PARENT INSIDE:
> You would have been better off doing it the other way, honey.

FUN-FREE CHILD INSIDE:
> You're right, I would have been better off doing it the other way, and next time I'll do it that way. But I'm still okay, even when I make a mistake.

THE LANGUAGE OF LOVE

Internal Conversation

QUESTION:
  How do I know I love myself or you?

ANSWER:
  By my willingness to make commitments
  to myself and others, and keep them.

NO RAPE!

13

No-Rape Analysis

This book has been devoted to the exploration and analysis of ways people conversationally rape each other throughout their lives, and the ways people can defend themselves from the traumatic consequences of such emotional language. In this final chapter I hope to end this book on a more uplifting note. I want to demonstrate how loving people think and talk about their feelings in a rational, non-emotional manner.

Emotional language includes repeated instances of *you should, you ought, you must* and *you have to*. We've seen many examples of *I can't, I'll try, I need,* and the unquantifiable question, *Why?* In contrast, the language of love is simple, and can be distilled down to a iterations of a single word: *I want..., I do not want..., I want you..., I do not want you....*

The language of love can be delivered in a dynamic fashion, or in a gentler way, with more feeling and more magnetism. The gentler way of "I want..." and "I do not want..." promotes the listener's thinking response.

When you ask your companion, "I want to go shopping tomorrow. Do you want to go with me?" the listener has the mental and emotional space to think freely through his or her decision and formulate a simple, direct response. In particular, this softer version works well with children who would be likely to react emotionally to a more direct, dynamic version.

"I want *you* to go shopping with me tomorrow. Do you want to go with me?" This is a more direct statement targeting a more specific response. It works well when the speaker wishes to convey both effectiveness and potency, and it puts immediate, though subtle, pressure on the listener for a positive response. Those men and women wishing to appear in charge of the situation would use this version of their desire.

Because it is more direct, however, this approach needs to be delivered with a bit more caution. Especially when used by a woman to address her man, an understanding of the gender energies underlying this statement needs to be fully taken into account. The male energy is by nature competitive, conquering and controlling. A woman who uses "*I* want *you* to..." will often trigger an unconscious competitive reaction. Even though the phrase is straightforward and honest, when a man sees himself as potent and responsive he may automatically rebel against a woman (or even another man who is not in a natural position of authority over him) who boldly instructs him with "I want you to..." to obtain her wants.

The wiser and more experienced woman has discovered that the magnetic use of loving language will generally get her more of what she wants. Couching the direct statement with a softening coda, such as "I want to... will you do it with me?" or "I do not want to... is that okay with you?" will often elicit a more favorable response from her man.

Knowing this simple approach to making requests allows everyone to have the power of choice. Gentle magnetism is available to pull a *thinking* response. It is more effective when dealing with the male of the species, whose brain is more oriented to logical thinking and rational exploration of consequences. Dynamic assertion, on the other hand, pulls a *feeling* response. It is arguably more effective when dealing with the female of the species, who is more often centered on her emotional state and her internal feelings. Although it obviates the necessity for constructing any logical argument to justify the request and speeds the listener's response, such a response may be either immediately positive or rebelliously negative.

Like a good public speaker, you need to know your audience to tailor your talk. You need to access your listener's rational capacities. This requires attention to their thoughts and feelings, which fortunately are constantly being demonstrated to you by their verbal and non-verbal language. When you as the speaker believe that your listener is in fact a rational loving person, you can talk straight. When the converse is true, and your listener is anxious and emotional, you will do well to understand that even with loving language, a negative reaction may occur. The person may not clearly hear what you are saying no matter how clearly you speak your request. This is where acceptance comes in.

Unconditional accepting love is demonstrated by patience when undertaking any negotiation. Too often, people *tolerate* others and the result is they use a language based on one-half love and one-half hate. This fifty-percent undermining exhibits four characteristics:

- A one-up, one-down attitude
- Impatience and abruptness with the other party
- Vague and imprecise commitments which seduce and rape both parties into causing pain when connections are not met or arrangements fall apart, and
- An unwillingness to ask for wants or cause pain by simply saying "No" to not-wants

All of these characteristics indicate a lack of self-centered love. They cement a foundation featuring a lack in sharing love with others.

We do not need to like or to approve of things as they are in our lives. And we are often willing to undertake many painful actions by deliberation when the price or prize is right. If you doubt that, just ask any World War II veteran about what a man is willing to do when the cause is sufficiently important. The sign of a truly mature person is a willingness to accept a certain degree of pain as a part of life, and a willingness to deal with pain rationally and not emotionally.

Men in particular will occasionally have difficulty dealing with women and children who are in some form of physical or mental pain. An emotional man will often deal with them by running away to drink, work or play compulsively. He may also attempt to bluster at them in noisy, intimidating, "macho" ways in order to scare them into shape. But the gentle and potent man *cherishes* his woman's and children's feelings, and uses his rational power of thought to assist in finding a solution if warranted.

Remember, though, that an expression of negative feelings is not always a plea for rescuing. Sometimes people, especially women, are just seeking a sympathetic ear so they can talk out their feelings and, ironically, now feel better. A man may automatically think he's being asked to resolve an unpleasant situation when, in fact, he really need only patiently hear it through.

I fully understand that people who continually talk about their feelings, and constantly dwell on the problems in their lives, are toxic and difficult to remain around for any period of time. And even love can have its limits. When you feel your own health and well-being is in jeopardy because the person you're with is overwhelming you, it's important that you take "evasive action" and leave the situation, either temporarily or permanently. Your greatest and most universal "want" is to want to be healthy, whole and in control of your own life and destiny.

Because that's the goal of all of us, even those who are mired in negative emotions and the trauma of their early conversational rapes, that's why it becomes so important to, whenever possible, help people filter their emotions through the rational capacities of the mind.

When emotions are channeled through thinking, especially thinking that uses the rational language of, for example, the WANT® Training system of Androgynous Semantic Realignment™ the emotions will ultimately lead to feelings that are positive, and motivate one into potent and assertive actions. And those actions will become the touchstone to attaining a healthy and whole life in which each individual is in control of his and her own destiny.

In summary, it has been my goal to demonstrate the theory behind communication which promotes straight talk. To be willing to speak clearly out of a concern for self and others is to promote the language of love in this world.

Dr. Pat Allen presents

Video and audio recordings of many of Dr. Pat Allen's seminars and teaching sessions on interpersonal communications, relationships and self-development, along with her best-selling books, are all available through the WANT® Institute, founded by Dr. Pat Allen. If you are unable to attend her seminars in person, viewing Pat on DVD or listening on CD is the next best thing. Some of her most potent teachings are now available for you to enjoy in your own home and to enhance your success in life and relationships, and all sales serve to support Pat's teaching and counseling efforts and to further the Mission of her WANT® Institute: "Educators of Effective Communication Strategies."

The following pages describe recordings and books which can be ordered directly over the internet by visiting the online **WANT Institute iStore** where you can purchase through our secure PayPal Shopping Cart, using either your credit card or your regular checking account.

TO ORDER ONLINE VISIT
WantInstitute.org/iStore

*To stay up to date with Pat's appearances on television and radio, please subscribe to the **Dr. Pat Allen Newsletter** and you will receive updates on the information presented in this book, information on her seminars and workshops, and free relationship advice and insights to help you with Dating, Relating and Enhancing Your Communication Skills and Self-Esteem. To subscribe, visit **DrPatAllen.com**.*

Note: The WANT® Institute is a 501(c)(3) nonprofit California corporation operating for educational, scientific and charitable purposes. Because of this, any educational products purchased may be fully tax deductible; and please consult with your financial consultant about the benefits of making a tax-deductible donation. The WANT® Institute is also a Federally Registered and Approved Health Care provider, National Provider Identifier (NPI) 1912034216. For more information and for a full curricula of classes available, visit us at:

Dr. Pat Allen

"The Secret"
Revealed the Power of the Law of Attraction!

"What The Bleep?"
Showed the Quantum Physics of Human Perception!

Now Dr. Pat Allen Has
"THE ANSWERS"
to Successful Sexual Relationships!

"THE ANSWERS from Dr. Pat Allen" DVD is a powerful introduction to the woman Oprah Winfrey calls the "Therapist, Comic Mother Superior" of human relationships, in a concise, first-ever collection of her insights and philosophies on the Dynamics of Human Interaction. In this highly charged overview, filled with information which she has learned from over 30 years of practicing couples counseling, her weekly jam-packed question-and-answer seminars, all-day workshops, and hundreds of appearances on TV and radio, Dr. Pat Allen gives you:

- *The tools to reverse negative feelings immediately.*
- *Insight into the 5 "Curses" of life, and their antidotes.*
- *A quintessential primer on how to Duty Date® successfully.*
- *The Power of Dr. Pat Allen's coveted negotiation tools.*
- *Dr. Pat Allen's foolproof formula on how to know if you really love someone.*

Speaking before an audience of over 700, Dr. Pat Allen explores the quantum physics of communication, and how it impacts the male and female energies in both sexes. She explains the three basic types of male-female relationships, the neurobiological mechanisms that lead women to repeatedly bond to the wrong men, the difference between "feminine" men who talk love, and masculine men who "do" love, and how both men and women can move from being chronic singles to lifelong mates.

Plus you get special **Bonus Features**: Be a "fly on the wall" in some of Pat's real-life therapy sessions where she helps couples stop games of seduction and intimidation and learn to negotiate with love; then create your own custom session using a unique Q & A database that allows you to have your own personal time with Dr. Pat Allen.

Do you want to live better and love better? The "secret" of life is really learning how to communicate effectively and with integrity. Dr. Pat Allen has *THE ANSWERS* that can help you prepare yourself for better love and a better life!

WANT® Training for Effective Living

CD & Workbook Set. 6 Dynamic Lessons on individual audio CDs — or choose our MP3 version with all 6 sessions on a single disk, perfect to copy to your iPod or other MP3 player. With either version you get nearly 5 ½ hours of in-depth instruction in Dr. Pat Allen's trademarked technique of WANT® Training that goes to the core of human communication...the Words That You Speak!

Dr. Pat Allen teaches you how to add powerful and lasting direction to your life and relationships by simply learning how to ask for what you want and saying "no" to what you don't want, using her rational, non-threatening system to communicate with integrity. Her system for personal growth uses Androgynous Semantic Realignment (a cognitive behavioral modification technique) to repair negative language habits. Because we think in words, changing those words changes how we think, and directly affects how we live.

With six clear, concise lessons Pat will train you how to use words as tools to get what you want out of life, to communicate lovingly, to confront both men and women in a respectful and cherishing manner, and to achieve fundamental self-esteem and restore physical and mental health:

- *How To Make A Decision Rationally, Not Emotionally.*
- *How To Speak Rationally and Assertively.*
- *Handling Emotional Confrontations Rationally.*
- *Re-Direct & Restructure Negative Habit Patterns Positively.*
- *Career Planning — How To Double Your Financial Success.*
- *Psychological Potency — Getting It and Using It.*

Set includes a **printed guidebook** filled with diagrams and life scripts to help you achieve personal success, psychological insight, and greater potency.

NOTE: The MP3 CD may not play on older CD players, but will be playable on any computer, as well as downloadable to your portable MP3 player or iPod. Guidebook is handy 5" x 8" size.

Dr. Pat Allen's "A Lifetime of Love"
(The Dummies' Guide to Relationships)

5-CD and Workbook Set. This is the companion piece and home study guide to Dr. Pat Allen's groundbreaking book on male-female relationships, *Getting To "I Do."* In this set of five audio CDs, she personally expands upon her basic principles of how to attract the right man or woman, why "equality" in a relationship dooms it to fail, how to get what you want from a man without ever asking for it, the three basic Types of Relationships, and the fundamental differences in what men and women need and expect from each other.

Each of these 30-minute lessons focus on one important area of communicating and applying language dynamics to Dating and Relating:

- *Masculine and Feminine Energies.*
- *Sex and Commitment.*
- *Conflicts and Communication.*
- *Sex and Obsessions.*
- *Phases of a Relationship.*
- *Flirting to Attract.*
- *Ten Secrets of Getting and Keeping the Right Partner.*
- *Suddenly Single: A Guide to Returning to the Dating Scene.*
- *Questions Most Often Asked by Men.*
- *Questions Most Often Asked by Women.*

The set also includes a study guide that contains charts and diagrams clarifying the way each of these principles can be applied to your life, questions for gaining greater self-understanding, and a series of humorous cartoons on the pitfalls of the Singles Life.

Dr. Pat Allen's "The Art of Relationships"

5-DVD and Communication Charts Manual Set. Dr. Pat Allen presents her complete seminar on "The Art of Loving" in which she goes in-depth into how to maintain respectful and cherishing relationships and answers the question: How can men and women learn to successfully relate in this new millennium of confusing sexual roles, cyber-dating and demands for crippling political correctness? Her observations on how male and female energies interact has helped her establish clear and concise techniques that either sex can use to achieve greater intimacy in any relationship — including erotic ones. And this goes for anyone: straight, gay, or lesbian.

In these presentations, Dr. Pat Allen explains how to set boundaries, deal with people who use "games" of intimidation, guilt and seduction, and communicate your needs and wants to your loved ones with integrity, by using her trademarked technique of Androgynous Semantic Realignment which has helped thousands of women to escape from unsatisfying relationships and finally make it to the altar:

- *Introduction to the Art of Relationships.* (1 hr)
- *Rational vs Emotional Behavior.* (1 hr 23 mins)
- *Communications Skills, Part 1.* (1 hr) *and Part 2* (1 hr 21 mins)
- *Setting Boundaries Verbally.* (1 hr 18 mins)
- *Special Bonus: Dream Analysis.* (26 mins)

These talks were filmed before a live audience on one of Pat's popular Alaskan Cruises for which people paid hundreds of dollars. The DVDs contain over 6 hours of insight, powerful communication techniques and her famous humor, and included is Dr. Pat Allen's "Communication Charts Manual" with diagrams that explain how Male and Female Energies interact in a relationship.

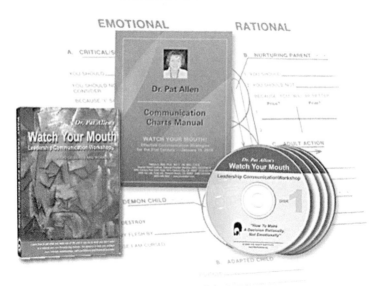

Dr. Pat Allen's "Watch Your Mouth"
Communication Strategies for the 21st Century

4-DVD and Communication Charts Manual Set. This 5-hour course is Pat's potent workshop on Leadership Communication Skills, that teaches you how to use words as tools, and how to get what you want in your business and personal life without hurting others. It's scientifically grounded in Cognitive Behavior Therapies and principles of Transactional Analysis, and uses techniques of Androgenous Semantic Realignment that Pat has developed during 40 years of counseling thousands of individuals, couples and families to achieve mutual harmony, spiritual growth, economic success and greater intimacy.

- **Androgenous.** You have aspects of both the masculine and the feminine within you. Discover which to emphasize in every individual communication situation.

- **Semantic.** Your actions are preceded by thoughts, and thoughts come as words. Learn to adjust your choice of words to suit any occasion, and think rationally about your feelings before you act. End the pain that comes from feeling, reacting—and then lamenting "Why did I do that?"

- **Realignment.** Energies in relationships must constantly adjust to meet situations that arise. Like the tires on your car, when your energies are not aligned you wear down and blow out. Get on track, rewrite your lifescript...and triumph in Act Three.

You can take charge of your life. Pat reveals the tools that allow you to take charge of the words you use in your thoughts, your speech, and in expressing your wants and not-wants to the people you live with, work beside, sell to, and share intimate sexual or family relationships. Learn the principles to create healthy, intimate relationships with mutual feelings of respect and cherishing, how to communicate clearly without ambiguity or ploys of gameyness, and learn the greatest secret of life: setting personal boundaries with love.

Dr. Pat Allen "Relationships in Recovery"
A Program for Persons With Addictive Personalities

10-DVD Set. We have three principle motivators: Sex, Money and Mind-Altering Chemicals, either produced in our bodies or drugs we buy. Dr. Pat Allen has personal experience with all three. A very special presentation of Pat's trademarked therapeutic advice for successful relationships, held at historic Wilson House in Vermont, birthplace of Bill W. (co-founder of AA), tailored to people who are in recovery from alcoholism or addictions to drugs, sex, or other forms of self abuse.

Over the course of three days she shared what she has learned about the unique aspects of sustaining positive relationships for people with addictive personalities, and the WANT Institute offers the complete weekend recorded on audio CD, courtesy of Glenn K Audio. 9 audio CDs, and bonus disk containing graphics in PDF format.

Talks include:

- *His Brain / Her Brain – Are They Different?*
- *Avoiding Conflict With Amigo Talk®*
- *Bring Your Tissues and Issues*
- *How To Make Decisions Rationally*
- *Pursuit of the Holy Grail in Sobriety*

Pat is an Addictions Specialist, Certified by the Harvard Medical School of Addictions. Pat's WANT Training and ASR Therapy is based on the psychological studies of Carl Jung, who helped define the 12-step principles of AA, and incorporates the work of Chuck C. (author of *A New Pair of Glasses*), Marilyn Bates, David Kersey, Dr. Charles Parker and even the stoic philosophy of Marcus Aurelius into an approach that is tailored perfectly toward persons who recognize they are disabled by physical or psychological aspects of addictions and seeking to overcome their weaknesses and get what they want, or need, out of life and their relationships. It's been a life-changing experience for many people.

Dr. Pat Allen's Groundbreaking Best-Seller
Getting To "I Do"

The Book That's Gotten Thousands of Women to the Altar!

HARDCOVER and PAPERBACK! Dr. Pat Allen's groundbreaking book is now in an astonishing 34th printing! Her jam-packed seminars in Los Angeles have resulted in thousands of marriages. Now you too can take advantage of this proven step-by-step program to put your love-life on the right track.

- *How to attract the right man.*
- *When you should make the first move...and when you should not.*
- *Why equality in a relationship may not be what you're looking for.*
- *Why sex before commitment is a bad deal.*
- *How to have sensational sex.*
- *What makes a man run away from a relationship.*
- *How to know when you're giving too much.*
- *How to get what you want without asking for it.*
- *What makes a man want to commit.*
- *How to BE ENGAGED TO THE RIGHT MAN WITHIN A YEAR!*

"Just what cupid ordered!"
—*Beverly Hills Today*

"Move over, Dr. Ruth!"
—*Los Angeles Magazine*

The Truth About Men
Will Set You Free...

...But first it'll p*ss you off!

Dr. Pat Allen & Don Schmincke reveal the *Science* Behind Sex and What Men Really Think About Sex and Dating

WARNING: This book will invade your comfort-zone. It was rejected by three top literary agents and dozens of publishers for being too controversial, edgy, or conflicting with current socially accepted norms. The male co–author originally had to adopt a pseudonym for self-protection from threats from enraged females. But the material is based on over 300 of the latest scientific research studies on how our species mates.

- *Why Denial Dooms Dating*
- *Why He Misinterprets Your Sexual Advances*
- *How To Be the Unfamiliar Female*
- *Where's a Guy's Real Sex Organ?*
- *Captivate Him with Darwin's 5-Step*
- *How To Avoid Being Seduced*
- *A Scientific Definition of "Love"*

If you're a woman, you may wind up throwing this book across the room in disbelief; yet it has delighted every male who's read it. Most have declared it the most factual book on male-female relationships ever written. And it espouses basic principles that, when applied, both genders found superior in producing successful and lasting relationships.

This book outlines Dr. Pat Allen's *Rules of Mating,* the most important of which is: "Those who didn't seek sex as the foundation of relationships are now extinct." If you want to learn The Truth About Men, be warned it'll probably tick you off at first...but it will definitely set you free. (Plan to read this book with a guy nearby just so you can keep asking him, "Is that how *you* think?")

"Duty Dating"
A film on life, love and a woman's quest for happiness

DVD. A feature-length romantic comedy about a smart and successful woman who does all the right things to marry the wrong man. Based on the teachings of nationally acclaimed author and lecturer Dr. Pat Allen, this uplifting film stars Lauren Sinclair ("Face Off") as a professional magazine stylist who manages to botch every potential sexual relationship and can't seem to understand what she's doing to sabotage herself, until her BFF takes her to a popular love and relationship specialist who clues her in to what it requires to create sustainable intimacy.

A heartwarming film that dramatizes the do's and don'ts of dating for the modern woman in her quest to find true love.

Duty Dating is a registered trademark of the WANT® Institute.

"Six (and a Half) Secrets of Love"
An Award-Winning Documentary
featuring Dr. Pat Allen and author John Gray

DVD. Dr. Pat Allen teams up with John Gray (best-selling author of *Men Are From Mars, Women Are From Venus*) in a giant therapy session to explore the quintessential secrets of love...and it turns out there are exactly 6 (and a half)!

John Gray talks about how hormones affect relationships and Dr. Pat Allen explains why hormones may make a man "pull back" from a woman he's becoming close to.

In addition, this film (winner of the 2007 Best Documentary at the Hollywood DV Film Festival) by Emmy-winning journalist Barbara Schroeder offers a treasure trove of wisdom to help lovers navigate their journey, including interviews with one couple who have been together for 68 years, and another woman who didn't find love until age 81! (43 mins.)

"Meet Dr. Pat Allen" Collection
Video Clips and Interviews Over the Years.

DVD. Great for anyone who wants to see samples of Pat's style of teaching, this historical "Meet Pat Allen, Ph.D., Best-Selling Author, Speaker, Psychotherapist, Communication and Relationship Expert" shows her in action in a variety of settings with clips from some of the TV programs that she's appeared on over the years, including the Oprah Winfrey show and CNN.

Originally prepared for Speakers Bureaus and event and meeting planners, this is also a great way to introduce people to Pat Allen, Ph.D. or to show to people who may be considering booking her for local speaking engagements, workshops for their employees, groups or organizations. The DVD also includes a 60-minute Keynote by Pat on "Being All You Can Be" which she delivered to the Annual WomanSage Conference (audio only).

"Highly Sensitive People"
Dr. Pat Allen's Androgynous "Alphas"

FULL HOUR ON DVD!

DVD. *Highly Sensitive People: An Introduction to the Trait of High Sensitivity* is a 65-minute presentation by Jim Hallowes, Executive Director of the WANT® Institute, delivered on Dr. Pat Allen's "The Art of Relationships" cruise to Alaska, and includes an overview of the trait, some common characteristics of HSPs, a review of famous people who have exhibited the Trait of High Sensitivity, along with tips and strategies and an HSP self-test. Dr. Pat Allen joins Jim for a special segment where she discusses her own experiences as a highly sensitive person, and offers an appreciation of Jim and his work in addressing this area.

Be sure to visit Jim's highly successful website <u>HighlySensitivePeople.com</u> for the latest news on HSP research, meet-up groups and Jim's speaking schedule.

Pat Answers Your Questions

- **Why Does My Life Suck?**
- **Why Don't I Have a Great Relationship?**
- **How Can I Tell if I'm Really in Love?**

The Answers Book From Dr. Pat Allen

Hollywood's beloved relationship counselor and licensed marriage, family and child therapist uses her 40 years of experience helping singles and couples, offering advice leavened with wit, humor and laser-like analysis that penetrates to the heart of life's most important issue:

Our Relationships With Others.

Cherrypicking examples from Pat's weekly stage shows, her appearances on Oprah, CNN and hit TV shows *"The Millionaire Matchmaker"* and *"I Love New York 2,"* Emmy-winning news reporter Barbara Schroeder has compiled a book full of startling anecdotes, testimonials, case studies and gem-like quotations that showcase the wisdom, insight and love that has endeared Dr. Pat Allen to the hearts of millions.

Discover this incredible woman's unique answers that will help you to solve life's toughest enduring questions.

You will live better and love better with *"The Answers From Dr. Pat Allen."*

The #1 quality men
are attracted to:

A HAPPY WOMAN

The #1 quality women
are attracted to:

**A MAN WHO KNOWS
HOW TO GIVE, PROTECT
AND CHERISH**

Listen to Dr. Pat Allen on Your iPod!

Dr. Pat Allen has been doing her regular Monday-night shows to packed houses for over 30 years at venues throughout Los Angeles (currently at the Odyssey Theatre in West L.A.), a presentation that *Los Angeles Magazine* has dubbed "Therapeutic Theater." Oprah Winfrey calls her the "Therapeutic, Comic Mother Superior," and notables like Marianne Williamson and comedian Yakov Smirnoff even drop by on many Mondays for a chance to watch her help individuals with insightful one-on-one counseling before a live audience in which Pat fields no-holds-barred questions about love, sex, and personal and erotic relationships.

We've started recording these exciting one-hour shows, in which Pat does a brief overview of her theories and then opens the floor to all comers, and they are available as MP3 downloads on the internet at **DRPATALLEN.COM**! Each show treats the relationship questions and problems of four to six individuals or couples, and demonstrates first-hand how communications expert Dr. Pat Allen's scientific principles can be applied to resolve any and all troubling interpersonal issues.

Are you tired of relationships that simply do not work? He won't commit; she won't surrender? Listen to Dr. Pat Allen explain how to get what you want out of life by learning how to correctly ask for it. "The Love Doctor," live and in-person, reveals what you must do to find and keep the man or woman of your dreams.

Printed in Great Britain
by Amazon